K

RECLAMING YOUR GOD-GIVEN
BIRTHRIGHT TO RULE ON EARTH

Born To Rule

RECLAMING YOUR GOD-GIVEN
BIRTHRIGHT TO RULE ON EARTH

CHRISTIAN SANTIAGO

Dedication

This book is dedicated to my co-ruler and wife, Chantal. You are so powerful that you constantly challenge me to be a better King and Priest. Thank you for being the Queen that you are.

CONTENTS

———————

 # Introduction

"Hey Mom, I want to ask you a question. Are you thinking about the end result right now?"

With audible sounds of sobbing, my mother said, "Unfortunately Christian, I am."

Here I was speaking to my mother on the phone because my father was in the hospital with high blood pressure. The issue was not the fact that my father battled this, which is something that he's dealt with for years, but it was the fact that his blood pressure was so astronomically high that he thought it was his time to see Jesus. What made everything worse was that my mother could not visit him due to it being during the coronavirus pandemic and he could not receive any visitors.

To put it into perspective about how high my father's blood pressure was when he was admitted into the hospital, a healthy blood pressure is 120/80. My father's pressure clocked in at a whopping 221/103, which is classified as a major health emergency. During the time I spoke to him about an hour before I spoke to my mother, he could only speak at the level of a whisper.

With him being a Puerto Rican, displaying apathy and quietness is foreign to him so I knew it was bad. I prayed with him and spoke with a level of boldness that his pressure the next day would drop to 140/80. I am not sure what came over me, but I knew I was still carrying it when I spoke to my mother later on.

"So Mom, has that end result happened yet? Has Dad died yet?"

Still sobbing profusely on the other end, "No Christian, he has not."

Pausing intently, I knew I had to ask my mother a difficult, yet serious question. I do not know why I thought this was a good question to ask, but I did anyways,

"So why are you crying right now and not taking dominion over these circumstances? If he passes away, we will all mourn together, but while he is still alive, we still have the opportunity to take authority over this situation."

My wife Chantal then felt led to pray for her heart, for renewed strength, and a greater sense of hope during that time. She then proceeded to ask my mother to pray for my father as if she was the one who had the power to change everything in this situation. Within a matter of seconds, my mother changed from being a woman who felt hopeless over her husband's situation to a warrior ready to do battle.

"Carlos Rene Santiago, you will not die, and you will get up from that hospital bed. As your wife, I do not allow you to leave yet. And every blood pressure or demonic force attacking his health must leave in the name of Jesus!"

By that time, I knew the inner woman inside of my mother had awakened and I instantly sensed that the best way to utilize this awareness was to put her on a three-way call with my father in the hospital. He answered immediately with the same faint whisper as before.

> "Hey Dad, I know you can barely talk so I want you to save your strength. Chantal and I were just talking with Mom and prayed for her. We then had her pray for you and take authority over this situation. We have her on the other line now and she's going to pray for you because I feel that she's the one with the authority to change everything in this situation."

What happened next shocked me. As my mother began to pray for my father's health, she started to pray for their future, not his high blood pressure! She prayed passionately about the future things God still had for them to do together and their assignment here on earth not being finished yet. After about seven minutes of impassioned prayer, I asked my father how he felt, and he started to laugh hysterically.

> "I felt life come back into me."

His volume returned back to normal and he started to crack his same old dad jokes with the explosive Puerto Rican energy like he always had in the past. After we talked for a bit, Chantal and I hung up the phone and stared at each other in amazement. The next day, my father's blood pressure dropped to 141/79 and he checked out a couple of days later with a 115/72, numbers for a healthy person who was in optimal shape.

As I took the next few days to process what just happened, I had a few questions. What possessed me to ask my mother to stop mourning and start taking praying with confidence? How did I recognize my mother was the one who had the power to change everything in this situation? Are there moments in my life that don't change or get better, not because God doesn't want it to, but because we don't take authority over it?

I share this impacting story with you because I discovered something about the identity of you and me. A powerful reality has been uncovered that has not been communicated much in our churches and modern world that would radically transform every believer on the earth. And that reality is this: God created each of us as rulers to lead this world in every way possible with the purpose of making it look like Heaven. In essence, we were born to rule.

This unrealized truth hit me as I began to study some of the more difficult passages in the Bible as soon as the coronavirus pandemic occurred. I began to wonder why God told Cain he could rule over sin (Gen. 4:6-7), dove into why the Lord told Joshua that he would make his own way prosperous (Joshua 1:8), and studied why Satan never received an objection from Jesus when he stated that every kingdom of the world was delivered to him (Luke 4:5-8).

All of these passages – and many more – led me to realize that when God made us, He had rulers in mind. He did not plan on making a reflection of Himself to be weak and mediocre, but to be powerful and for them to dominate. It was these truths that caused me to believe my father could be healed if we took authority. Since high blood pressure does not exist in Heaven, I sensed the leading to take authority over it and exercise the birthright we've been given by God that was restored through the sacrifice and resurrection of King Jesus. And as you already know, it worked, and God healed him.

That's the thing about the Scriptures: they are no good if we are not willing to put in practice what is revealed to us. Knowledge of them is not enough. We must be willing to take risks to see the truths of Scripture be actualized in our world, especially if we are going to make this earth look like Heaven. And when we do that, we cannot be surprised when the supernatural begins to become a common occurrence.

But you need to know something important if you are going to see these same results happen for you: there must be a willingness to embrace a fresh identity of who you *really* are. This new discovery will cause you to put away a low self-image, see yourself as the ruler you really are, create an insatiable hunger for the Word of God, and embrace a greater responsibility for the world we have been entrusted with by our Father.

For us to do this, however, a realization must occur. It is one that is not easy to accept nor receive. The realization is that we have made a choice to live out our lives on a half-truth instead of the full truth. We have chosen to settle for just a portion of who we are instead of all that we are. You're probably questioning, In what way have I built my life on a half-truth? What part of my Christian walk has been established on a lie?

The lie we have settled for believing is this: the only thing Jesus sought to restore was intimacy with God because that's what was lost in the Garden. Because of this lie, we have declared the entirety of the Gospel is for Man to regain his relationship with God and nothing else.

Yes, our intimacy with God was interrupted in the Garden due to Adam's disobedience, but intimacy wasn't the main thing he lost. If that were true, how could these relationships be formed in the Old Testament?

- Enoch walked closely with God and being taken up (Genesis 5:24)
- Abraham being known as a "friend of God" (Isaiah 41:8, James 2:23)
- Moses spoke with God "as a man to a friend face-to-face" (Exodus 33:11)
- David being "a man after God's own heart" (1 Samuel 13:14, Acts 13:22)

- Solomon had direct conversations with God (2 Chronicles 1:7)
- Isaiah peered into the direct counsel of God (Isaiah 6)
- Jonah fought directly with God over Nineveh (Jonah 4)
- Job spoke face-to-face with God in a whirlwind (Job 38)

And the list goes on. If the main thing that was lost in the Garden was intimacy, then how did these men in the Old Testament have the opportunity to connect with God on a personal and intimate level? Why did God want Israel to be a "kingdom of priests" unto Him so everyone could have access to His presence, not just Aaron's lineage (Ex. 19:6)? Could it be because there was something else lost in the Garden that was just as important, if not *more* important?

Your Rulership Identity

We have sorely understated the power of the Gospel by limiting it to just one focus. Many have proclaimed that accepting the work of the Cross is the only thing people have to look forward to in their Christian walk. This proclamation has unfortunately left many empty and frustrated thinking to themselves, "I'm saved. Now what?"

Usually when this question is asked, the primary responses have to do with now telling people about Jesus, attending weekly services, and living a good moral life waiting to get to Heaven. But this could not be further than the truth. What our Savior and King wanted for us had nothing to do with people's good church (or synagogue) attendance nor establishing a religion. He never even preached this. His desire was for us to be redeemed so we would actualize His Kingdom on the earth. He never wanted us to wait for Heaven, but to bring Heaven down.

In the current climate of Christianity, there's been mainly one focus: accepting Jesus as Savior through His work on the Cross. This is great, but many have missed that the purpose of the Cross wasn't to only save us from Hell, but to make us holy for the Holy Spirit to fill us for the purpose of ruling again, and Heaven manifesting on earth through us. In simplest terms, the sacrifice of Jesus was saving us *from* Hell and *to* the present reality of the Kingdom of Heaven.

This next statement may shock you, but we were more than just sinners needing to be saved by grace, we were rulers and children of God who became sinners through disobedience to His laws. The mission of our King was not solely to save sinners, but to restore rulers back to their place of authority on the earth who were deceived by Satan. If we peer into the book of Genesis, we can see that when the Divine Creator chose to create mankind to live in the world He formed out of nothing, He declared a purpose for their existence.

> Then God said, "Let Us make man in Our image, according to Our likeness; let them have **dominion** over the fish of the sea, over the birds of the air, and over the cattle, over all the earth and over every creeping thing that creeps on the earth." (Genesis 1:26, NKJV)

God Almighty designed and built Man to function as a ruler. This is why when things get out of control in our lives, it causes our souls to malfunction through anger, worry, anxiety, etc. All of this occurs because we were created to rule every area of our lives. Adam, and every other person that followed in his lineage, was given God's image and likeness to affirm that truth.

How does God's image and likeness affirm this truth? The answer lies in defining what image and likeness means. The first word – image – can be defined as essence, which simply means same substance. If we are to rule and have dominion over the physical realm of earth like God does in the spiritual realm of Heaven, we must be created with the same spiritual DNA as Him. Essentially, God created us with the same spiritual DNA as Him and then put us in a dirt body.

The second word – likeness – can be defined as the ability to function like the thing it represents. During my second semester of my freshman year in college, my closest friends met my father for the first time. Just as you heard prior about Puerto Ricans, we are really energetic and passionate.

After thirty minutes of his explosive energy and hysterical laughing, one of my friends turned to me with a big smile on her face saying, "Now it makes sense why you are the way you are." I had no words for that statement because it was true; I was made in my father's likeness and functioned like him.

You see, all of mankind was intended to function like God in every way. We were meant to operate on this earth in such a way that when all of creation saw us, they would actually see Him. Nothing was ever meant to subdue or dominate us, not even Hell itself. Rulership is our heritage and birthright through our identity as sons and daughters of the Most High. After Man was established as a ruler on earth, you will see that sonship follows.

> So God created man in **His own image**; in the **image of God** He created him; male and female He created them. (Genesis 1:27, NKJV)

As we will talk about later in more detail, God made Man out of His own seed. He spoke to the world to bring forth its potential and then spoke to Himself to bring forth His own potential. Even Adam is called the son of God in Luke's genealogy account to echo this truth (Luke 3:38). When our rulership identity is expressed through the affirmed soul of being a son or daughter of God, we will not misuse the authority we have been entrusted with on this earth.

If we still possess the insecurity of an orphan frantically searching for affirmation and approval, then we can fall into the trap of misrepresenting or distorting the image we are supposed to reflect. This is precisely why I would encourage you to buy books that speak to the spirit of sonship or overcoming the orphan spirit as a supplement to this roadmap to living out your rulership birthright.

I share all of this in this lengthy introduction to shed light on the fullness of our identity in God's eyes and how Jesus came to restore it so we could take back this world from Satan's influence. As the Gospel has been preached, there have been many books written about the power of the Cross and how it allows us to be forgiven and filled with the Holy Spirit. There are also plenty more that speak about sonship and living this life as a son or daughter of the King instead of with an orphan spirit. But there are very few, if not any, books that are written about our original identity as rulers.

It is for this reason that I am inspired by the Holy Spirit to write about in these upcoming pages. We were sanctified, filled with the Holy Spirit, and made children of God for a reason – and that reason is for *rulership*. If we do not know the 'why' behind a thing we do or a process we partake in, then, after a while, it will have no meaning or possess any authentic power in our lives. And by no means did God create you and me to be anything less than the rulers we are.

Garden Government

Have you ever wondered why when children are little, they imagine themselves to be superheroes and possess unique abilities? Whether it is a little boy wanting to teleport or a little girl wanting to use the power of mind control, they instinctively believe they are strong, powerful, and possess a desire to lead. Even some of the most loving and shy children possess this spirit of leadership in them.

When I was a children's pastor, there was a girl named Abby, who was very sweet, loved Jesus, and was a pastor's kid. She lived and breathed the Church and loved every moment of it. She was never rude and was always soft-spoken.

But even with her soft-spoken nature, there was that spirit of leadership inside of her that's dormant in every child, and, consequently, in every human being. This was displayed when she wanted a lot of candy.

It was a Tuesday afternoon when Abby came into the church offices with her joy and smile. Everyone greeted the lovely and happy fourth grader, who cared about everyone she came into contact with. Her mom came in behind her and as soon as she took one step inside the room, Abby came running to her.

"Mom!"
"Yes, Abby?"
"Can I have some?"

As she asked, her arm pointed towards the opposite corner of the room where we had jars of candy sitting.

"Yes, but not too much"
"Yes! Thank you!"

With a full smile, she ran over and open the jar to grab a handful of mini Snickers. I was watching the entire exchange and noticed how much candy she had in her hand. I thought this was a perfect time to experiment something I recently learned.

"Hey Abby!"

"Hey Pastor Christian! Look at all my candy!"

"Wow, that's a lot of candy. Do we want to maybe put one back? I mean, Mommy did say not too much."

"........."

I could tell that with her silence, she was thinking about what to say. After a few seconds, she gave the response I thought she would – first through a whisper, then with a shout.

"You're not the boss of me."

"What did you say, Abby? I didn't hear you."

"I said, you're not the boss of me!"

It was in that moment that I started to laugh uncontrollably for a few moments because I was so proud of her.

"Great job, Abby. I'm proud of you. Enjoy your candy."

"Thank you, Pastor Christian!"

And with that, she gave me a high-five with the one free hand she did have and ran to the nearest table to enjoy it. It was in that moment that it confirmed in my heart that what is innate in every human being is the spirit of dominion.

Garden Kings & Queens

When Adam was created on the sixth day, he already had a mandate on his life. His purpose was set by God before he was formed on earth. No, his primary purpose had nothing to do with singing songs to God, nor living a good moral life. In fact, in Genesis 1:26-28, God makes it very clear what Adam's purpose was and all of mankind.

> Then God said, "Let Us make man in Our image, according to Our likeness; **let them have dominion** over the fish of the sea, over the birds of the air, and over the cattle, over all the earth and over every creeping thing that creeps on the earth." ... Then God blessed them, and God said to them, "Be fruitful and multiply; fill the earth and **subdue it;** have dominion over the fish of the sea, over the birds of the air, and over every living thing that moves on the earth." (Genesis 1:26, 28, NKJV)

God's purpose for Adam, Eve, and all of Man would be to have dominion over the earth. He placed on them the divine authority to be the kings and queens of their domain.

Their leadership would be one of a relational-rulership, where the King of the country they were representing would walk with them in close partnership and teach them how to rule like Him.

This is vital to understand because if we are talking about the purpose of mankind, not many people know that they were born to rule. They do not know their first inheritance is that of Garden kings and queens. It is evident when people take the place of a victim and choose to blame everything on their outside circumstances instead of taking responsibility for their responses to their situations. If we realized we were born to lead and rule, we would already squash much of the low self-esteem, poverty mentality, and victimhood many Christians within the Church possess.

Being a Latino male myself, this mindset was evident in my upbringing. I was never told I was born to rule or to be a king under the King of Kings (Revelation 1:6). Because of this, I didn't do a good job ruling my emotions, heading my home correctly when I first got married, and overcoming obstacles in front of me, even though I was more than a conqueror (Romans 8:37). I used to get angry at other people for their starting point, without realizing that my mindset hindered me from making progress in my own life.

This does not negate that some people have a less fortunate starting point than others. What is incredible though is in the Kingdom, it is less about your starting point and more about your ending point. Even the Apostle Paul said he wanted to focus on pressing ahead instead of looking back,

> Brethren, I do not count myself to have apprehended; but one thing I do, **forgetting those things which are behind** and **reaching forward to those things which are ahead**, I press toward the goal for the prize of the upward call of God in Christ Jesus. Philippians 3:13-14 (NKJV)

What's noteworthy about those verses is that in the preceding ones he speaks about letting go of his starting point, which was a very beneficial one. He studied under Gamaliel, one of the most prominent teachers of his day, and advanced more quickly than any of his peers.

He experienced rapid success in all that he did and yet, he counted his rich starting point as of no value compared to what was ahead. If Paul received inspiration by the Holy Spirit to let go of his rich starting point, how much more should we do the same, especially those of us who've had an unfavorable starting point?

While that may seem hard for you, you need to know this startling truth: it is only difficult to let go of your past if you have accepted your identity as a victim rather than a ruler. And if this is hard for you, then that's why I wrote this book. The Holy Spirit has inspired me more than ever in this season to speak about the things that have kept the Body in chains and that have hindered Her from being fully unleashed in the world.

As hard or completely different as these truths may be to hear, stick with me to the end. You will realize that what we've been told was, in fact, a part of the truth, but it wasn't the whole counsel of God. But for now, let's return back to the king and queen of Eden. As we've noted earlier, the primary purpose of Man given by God Himself was to rule and have dominion over the earth and the works of His hands. Even David says this in Psalm 8,

> What is man that You take thought of him, And the son of man that You care for him? Yet You have made him a little lower than **God**, And You crown him with glory and majesty! You make him to **rule over the works of Your**

> **hands**; You have put **all things** under his feet, (Psalm 8:4-6, NASB)

This declaration of us being made a little lower than God and given rulership over the work of His hands by King David through the Holy Spirit communicates to us that we are more powerful than anyone has told us. Even in Genesis 1 when God created Man, He did so in such a way that Man came from out from the inside of the Divine Creator.

During the creation process in Genesis 1:11-12, God had already made the earth, seas, sky, night, and day. What's shocking is when God wanted trees, forests, mountains, fruit, and vegetables to be made, He didn't create them, He spoke to the earth to produce them.

> Then God said, "**Let the earth bring forth** grass, the herb that yields seed, and the fruit tree that yields fruit according to its kind, whose seed is in itself, on the earth"; and it was so. **And the earth brought forth** grass, the herb that yields seed according to its kind, and the tree that yields fruit, whose seed is in itself according to its kind. And God saw that it was good. (Genesis 1:11-12, NKJV)

In other words, God created the earth and then placed the seed of potential inside of it. Instead of creating something separate from the earth to place on it, He just spoke to the earth to produce what was dormant inside of it. He used His words to extract the earth's internal potential. Even in Genesis 1:20 and 1:24, God begins with speaking to the potential of the seas and earth first, then the creation process follows.

If we follow the narrative properly as it has been lined up, God then turns His attention from what was before Him to what was inside of Him. Just as He spoke to the earth and seas before producing what was inside of them, God spoke to Himself to produce what was inside of Him!

> Then God said, "Let Us make man in **Our image**, according to **Our likeness**; let them have dominion over the fish of the sea, over the birds of the air, and over the cattle, over all the earth and over every creeping thing that creeps on the earth." (Genesis 1:26, NKJV)

Adam is a product not just of the dust of the earth, but also of the Divine Creator Himself. Mankind is God's potential on the earth. The first man to live was created out of the seed of God and came out of Him directly!

Because Adam was created out of the very seed of God, he was endowed with the spirit of dominion – which is the act of dominating a specific domain. The same qualities our Father possesses, He has placed inside of His children.

Unfortunately, what has occurred are two things: we have either distorted it or suppressed it. Those who seek dominion without a surrendered heart to Christ have misrepresented the spirit of dominion.

They have sought after power, riches, or influence to create the world as *they* see fit instead of how God sees fit, all the while bringing oppression to people of the second group. If the distortion of the spirit of dominion can occur, then suppression of it can happen too. This is when people believe less than who they have been made to be.

They settle for anything life gives them and then blame God if things do not work out favorably for them. Choosing to settle for a lesser life allows people who distort the spirit of dominion to oppress them. The second group of people may fight back at first, but eventually, they will succumb to complaining or bickering due to suppression of their initial design.

But when a heart is fully surrendered to walk with Christ, just as Adam walked with God before the Fall, and embraces the mandate of dominion on it, then that person will have the supernatural authority and power to shape the world as King Jesus sees fit! Adam walked in the spirit of dominion and authority like that of his Father that even God stepped back and allowed Adam to name everything He brought him.

> Out of the ground the Lord God formed every beast of the field and every bird of the air and **brought them to Adam** to see what he would call them. And whatever Adam called each living creature, **that was its name.** (Genesis 2:19, NKJV)

Since Adam walked closely with God and He made it clear that Man would have dominion over the earth, the Divine Creator gladly stepped back and allowed His seed to exercise what he received from his Father. To go even further, God does not interfere with Adam and Eve's dominion until after the Fall, until after the Holy Spirit left from the inside of them due to their sin. Want to know why? It is because of God's first design for Man when He created him.

> Then God said, "Let Us make man in Our image, according to Our likeness; let **them** have dominion over the fish of the sea, over the birds of the air, and over the cattle, over all the earth and over every creeping thing that creeps on the earth." (Genesis 1:26, NKJV)

Did you notice the essential word in that verse? Well, if you didn't, that's okay because I never did either until someone showed me. The critical word in that verse is "them."

The Creator explicitly declared that when He created Man, He wanted "them" to have dominion over the earth. It meant that God had given His authority to Man for them to rule the ground they walked on. He would not override their dominion unless they asked or if it got so bad that He had to intervene Himself.

In other words, if things went wrong on the earth, it wasn't God's fault, it was ours. He gave us the responsibility to rule and lead the world in the same way He ruled Heaven. Even Psalm 115:15-16 says this,

> May you be blessed by the Lord, who made heaven and earth. The heaven, even the heavens, are the Lord's; **But the earth He has given to the children of men**. (Psalm 115:15-16, NKJV)

This verse proclaims the endowment of responsibility and management, not ownership. In ancient times, kings would own everything in their domain (kingdom means "king's domain") and therefore would possess sovereign and ultimate control but would delegate authority to others for them to make decisions in their place.

Just because God gave Man responsibility and management over the earth does not void His sovereignty. In fact, God still intervened numerous times in the Bible when Man stopped ruling the way He saw fit. But the overriding principle is the same: Adam and Eve were created in the Garden to rule and God would not step in to take that away.

When our view of ourselves changes from being a victim to a ruler and we begin to assume responsibility for our homes, cities, regions, states, and countries, then the spirit of dominion and rulership implanted inside of us from the beginning of time will come out. We will step out to influence and lead our world the way the King over us leads His Kingdom. After all, we are Heaven's representatives on earth! Heaven is not weak, does not shrink back, and is always advancing. We should be the same.

This truth of how taking responsibility changes your world has become even more apparent with being married to a former interior designer. My wife, Chantal, was an interior designer in Australia for seven years. All of the experience, love, and passion for everything home-related is inside of her because of this seven-year period. It is such a part of who she is that she assumes full responsibility for making our home look beautiful.

She chooses all of the colors, cares about what types of pillows we have on our bed, the fabric of the couch, and even how it smells. Even though sometimes it frustrates me in the moment because she may be very picky about certain furniture, I am genuinely grateful later on after everything is set in place because of her deciding to take responsibility for our home.

I bet there are certain things in your life that if you took more responsibility over and developed that mindset, you could produce excellence in that area. When it comes to personal finances or preaching, I take personal responsibility over the results and that is why my family has seen abundant fruit from my preaching and our personal finances. If God has given us the blessing to flourish in whatever area we take full responsibility for, how would our world look like if the children of God exercised their spirit of dominion and responsibility to transform it?

It is because of this declaration in Genesis that if we see unsolved problems in our world, it has less to do with

God's actions and more to do with our inactions. God honors His own word and our rulership so much that instead of doing everything Himself, He fills us with His Spirit to work through us and collaborate with us.

Rulership and Servanthood

There are some who are going to grasp this message and use their newly discovered position of authority to bring healing to their world and the world around them. Then there are others who will try to use this message to rule over other people. Isn't that what rulers do – rule over others? Unfortunately, those who are of the second group did not properly read what God spoke in the beginning about the purpose of mankind.

> Then God said, "Let Us make man in Our image, according to Our likeness; let them have dominion **over the fish of the sea, over the birds of the air, and over the cattle, over all the earth and over every creeping thing that creeps on the earth**." (Genesis 1:26, NKJV)

The declaration of dominion and rulership over all of mankind included all of the birds, the animals, the things that creep on the earth, and anything else that seeks to subdue them. What is excluded in this pronouncement is the assignment to rule over *other image bearers*. In other words, God never instructs Man to rule over each other, only the things against them.

The reason is simple. God – being a good and perfect Father – knows that sibling rivalry and competition destroys families more than it builds them. It tears them apart more than it binds them together, so His declaration in the beginning was actually Him acting as a Father establishing what the family business would be about. That His children would work together instead of against each other to rule His property.

Even Jesus spoke about this with His disciples. His heart for them, and for everyone who would come after them, would be for them to exercise their rulership identity properly. To live rightfully as a king or queen under God means that **we rule things and serve people.** This is displayed as our King gives His followers Kingdom wisdom about wielding their authority.

> But Jesus called them to Himself and said, 'You know that the rulers of the Gentiles lord it over them, and those who are great exercise authority over them. **Yet it shall not be so among you**; but whoever desires to

become **great** among you, let him be your **servant**. And whoever desires to be first among you, let him be your slave — just as the Son of Man did not come to be served, but **to serve**, and to give His life a ransom for many.' (Matthew 20:25-28, NKJV)

Did you notice that Jesus never discouraged His disciples for achieving or desiring greatness? That's because He wanted them to be great. The only issue was that He had to redefine what greatness looked like for them. He knew exactly how we were designed from the very beginning and intimately understood how our dominion mandate should be carried out.

We were created to dominate everything except other image bearers. He communicated this by showing that greatness is reached when we accept our assignment of servanthood towards people. When we serve others, they will gladly lend their power to serve us back or use it to serve others. As the cycle of serving continues, more of this earth will begin to reflect Heaven because we will have more giving than taking.

This is why the greatest and most profitable businesses are ones that serve the most people. The most prominent doctors are the ones who discovered the medical breakthroughs that eradicated a disease that used to wipe out multitudes of people.

Songs, books, and paintings that are famous throughout time are ones that touch many people across generational, cultural, and socioeconomic lines. If you want to be great and have one billion dollars, go solve a one-billion-person problem. Go be a servant to all and watch the words of our King come to pass.

But due to the sinful nature we inherited through the Fall, we have flipped the order from ruling things and serving people to ruling people and serving things. Instead of becoming someone who uses our power to aid people, many have used it to lord it over them. They then begin to serve things rather than ruling them. Their lust for power, platform, money, position, image are all by-products serving those things instead of taking them captive to the obedience of Christ.

Do not be deceived into believing that recognizing your position as a ruler means you can see yourself above others, position yourself higher than them, or exercise your power for them to serve you instead of you serving them. We have been called to take on the mandate of both rulership and servanthood. King Jesus was the model of what it means to be a Servant-King. Now we get the opportunity to learn under His example.

Taking Back Our Authority

When God said that Man would have dominion over the results of the earth, He did not want to break that. The reason for this is because God is a King. When Kings issue decrees or give edicts, they seek to fulfill every part of that word or else they would be proven a liar and be deemed untrustworthy. This is why His word does not return to Him without accomplishing its purpose (Isaiah 55:11) and why kings like Darius or Herod had to fulfill their decrees even when they did not want to (Daniel 6:12-16; Matthew 14:6-10).

To show His fulfillment of this word spoken in Genesis, God chose to make a strategic decision: instead of changing everything from Heaven with a different decree, He chose to come as a man Himself. If one Adam lost our ability to properly rule and have dominion over the earth, we needed

41

a second Adam to get it back (1 Corinthians 15:47). After the last Adam rose from the dead, his first words in His commission to the disciples were,

> And Jesus came and spoke to them, saying, "All **authority** has been given to Me in heaven and on earth." (Matthew 28:18, NKJV)

Jesus spoke about regaining the authority that was lost in the Garden when Adam and Eve sinned. You see, when Man fell in the garden through disobedience, they did not lose their ability to rule and have dominion over the earth, they just allowed someone else, Satan, to have access to their power to rule.

Being the only beings to have dominion over the earth, every spirit being – whether from the kingdom of Heaven or the kingdom of darkness – wants access to our power to either free or enslave others. As the Holy Spirit left from indwelling inside of Adam and Eve when they sinned, the one who had greater access was Satan. This allowed him to rule Cain's heart to kill his brother and allowed him to have authority over cities, regions, and countries. If you don't believe me, look at Luke's account of the devil's temptation of Jesus,

> Then the devil, taking Him up on a high mountain, showed Him all the kingdoms of the world in a moment of time. And the devil said to Him, "All **this authority** I will give You, and their glory; for this has been **delivered to me**, and I give it to whomever I wish. Therefore, if You will worship before me, all will be Yours." (Luke 4:5-7, NKJV)

When I first read this verse, it disrupted my theology heavily. It messed up everything I believed, especially when I looked at the response of Jesus.

> And Jesus answered and said to him, "Get behind Me, Satan! For it is written, 'You shall worship the Lord your God, and Him only you shall serve." (Luke 4:8, NKJV)

Did you notice that Jesus never refuted the fact that Satan had been delivered authority over all of the kingdoms of the world? If you read it carefully, Jesus solely pointed to worshiping God only. This is because He knew His destiny was to take back all of the authority Satan received. He was just going to take it back by going through the Cross, not by bowing down to him. If you don't believe me that Satan possessed authority over this world, look at our King's words in John 12,

> 'Now is the judgment of this world; **now the ruler of this world will be cast out.** And I, if I am lifted up from the earth, will draw all peoples to Myself.' This He said,

43

signifying by what death He would die. (John 12:31-33, NKJV)

The ruler of this world will be cast out? Isn't God the ruler of this world? Jesus even said the work of the Holy Spirit is to bring judgment to the ruler of this world.

> Of judgment, because the **ruler of this world** is judged. (John 16:11, NKJV)

Even the Apostle Paul says this about Satan when writing to the Ephesian Church,

> And you He made alive, who were dead in trespasses and sins, in which you once walked according to the course of this world, according to the **prince of the power of the air**, the spirit who now works in the sons of disobedience, (Ephesians 2:1-2, NKJV)

Jesus called him the ruler of this world, Paul calls him the prince of the power of the air, and Satan himself said the kingdoms of the world were delivered to him. This begs the question: who gave him this authority over the earth?

We did. That's right – the children of Man gave him the authority placed on us. Satan became the ruler of this world because when we sinned in the Garden, the Holy Spirit left us, and we no longer gave Heaven access to work through the power we were given. If the house is empty, then evil spirits will take advantage of it to occupy it (Matthew 12:44-45, Genesis 4:7).

Since men did not live under the laws of Heaven, they allowed the lawlessness of hell to run rampant into the world. And due to the power we were already given, this allowed Satan to become the ruler of this world. But another unanswered question comes up: isn't God the ruler of this world? Well, yes and no.

Yes, because God is the King and owner of this world. He rules over the universe, and His purposes cannot be thwarted. And no, because there is something that exists known as delegated rulership.

In ancient times, especially during the Roman empire, delegated rulership was commonplace. King Agrippa II - the one who heard Paul's testimony in Acts 26 - ruled in Judea on behalf of Emperor Nero at the time. He did not have the ultimate and sovereign rule over his area or domain. Still, he was entrusted with the power of his king to make decisions for his region that lined up with the interest of the homeland.

The Emperor would not interfere or intervene unless it was under dire circumstances or if a rebellion broke out that could topple the entire empire. As for us, God has made us His delegated rulers of this world. He's given us His image and made us into His likeness that whatever happens in this world is our responsibility. We have so much power in this world that even our words can create life or death (Proverbs 18:21).

Because God will not void His own words (Matthew 24:35) and will never lie (Numbers 23:19), He decided that to have access to the delegated rulership of Man He gave them, He chose to come as a man Himself. His mission was to bridge the gap that caused us to not live with the indwelling of the Holy Spirit – sin.

Sin always had a hold on us, and the sacrifices of bulls and lambs were only a temporary measure. The only way the debt of sin could be paid, and the holiness of our King be satisfied is if the traitors themselves would be punished. Kings will not allow traitors into their kingdom because their very presence could sow more seeds for rebellion. Yeast is the picture that is often depicted of this reality (Matthew 16:6; Galatians 5:7-9).

This is precisely why Jesus became sin so that we could become the righteousness of God (2 Corinthians 5:24). This is why Paul said he was crucified with Christ, and he no longer lives, but Christ lives in him (Galatians 2:20). Our sinful, traitorous selves needed to completely die for the wrath of our Holy King to be satisfied. Once sin was taken care of, and we became the righteousness of God, then our minds, hearts, and souls became worthy places for the Holy Spirit to dwell. After all, the Holy Spirit only dwells in holy vessels.

Why does all this matter? Because your entire walk with Christ and your life on earth will be defined by one word: *access*. That's what this spiritual war is about. It is all based on which kingdom will have access on earth through men. Access is so important that we are commanded to take all thoughts captive that are contrary to Christ (2 Corinthians 10:5-6), to focus on every godly and good thing (Philippians 4:8), and to not allow the enemy to gain a foothold in our lives (Ephesians 4:25-27).

Everything is about access. If we allow the Holy Spirit to possess total control in our lives, then we will not allow the flesh to possess power. If we allow the flesh to gain complete access into our lives, then the Holy Spirit will not be able to and the devil will take advantage. Paul himself knew this battle was about access in that he had to forgive someone who attacked him because he did not want Satan to have control over his heart.

> Now whom you forgive anything, I also forgive. For if indeed I have forgiven anything, I have forgiven that one for your sakes in the presence of Christ, lest **Satan should take advantage of us**; for we are not ignorant of his devices. (2 Corinthians 2: 10-11, NKJV)

If Paul was not ignorant of Satan's schemes and devices, you should not be either. Make no mistake: the reason access is of primary importance is because you are more powerful than anyone ever told you. The spirit of dominion inside of you is so dynamic that both Heaven and Hell are battling for you.

Remember this, though: you can only give access to one at a time. We either give Satan access through sin or the Holy Spirit access through surrender. My heart for you is to take the spirit of dominion you have been given and surrender it entirely to the Spirit of God. Allow Him to shape your heart and let Him place a burden of responsibility within your heart for your neighborhood, your city, and your home.

It's time you embraced the power implanted within and use it to expand the influence of the Kingdom of Heaven. It's time you viewed yourself as a ruler instead of a victim. It's time you rose up to a place of influence in your community, so the fate of our cities will not be decided by people who have not given access to the Holy Spirit.

As you go out with the mindset of dominion, you will notice opportunities will open up more naturally than before, and your impact will increase exponentially. God will use you to impact influential people in your area and industry for eternity. This will cause more lives to be changed by Heaven as a result of their decision-making now being inspired by the Holy Spirit.

Take up your mantle of rulership. Take responsibility for your world. Partner with the King of Kings to destroy the works of the devil. Embrace your calling to be a Garden King or Queen.

You have the power to change more than you think and, when partnered with the Holy Spirit, you possess even more power. It's about time you discovered your original design. It's about time you knew the real "YOU." Now let's live like it. The best way we can do this is by taking back our rightful place.

Key Principles

1. What is innate inside every man, woman, and child is the spirit of dominion.

2. God's primary intention purpose for Man was for them to have dominion, or control, over the earth.

3. The greatest way mankind can exercise their dominion power is through relational-rulership with God.

4. Every human being's heritage is that of a king and queen in Eden.

5. In the Kingdom, it is less about your starting point in life and more about your ending point.

6. Mankind is God's potential on the earth.

7. Without Christ, we either distort or suppress the spirit of dominion.

8. Whatever we take responsibility for flourishes and whatever we pass on to someone else will die.

9. Unsolved problems in our world have less to do with God actions and more to do with our inactions.

10. We are made to rule things and serve people, not the other way around.

11. Your entire Christian walk will be defined by one word: access.

12. We either give access to Satan through sin or the Holy Spirit through surrender.

Taking Back Our Rightful Place

"Can you just leave me alone?"

Her ocean-blue eyes gazed deeply into mine, and she asked this question. With frustration in her tone, I could tell this was more of a command rather than a request. I had a choice to make in that moment: do I push her even further, or do I step away to avoid further conflict? As tough as more conflict may seem, I already made the decision to go forward no matter how tense the situation may become.

"No, I will not. Nothing you say is going to convince me to stop."

As soon as those words left my mouth, she knew that I made my decision. She could sense the fierce determination in my voice and could see it plainly in my eyes. My heart began to race gearing up for what could be a big argument. My mind calculated at warp speed about all the different things I could say to convince her of my viewpoint. Then, within moments of my determined response, her eyes softened and filled with tears.

"Why do you believe in me so much?

And with that question, her cry for affection and love was heard as she sank into my arms for a big hug. She laid her head on my shoulder as I spoke these words to her.

"It's because of what I see in you. You have so much wisdom and power inside of you that the worst thing you can do is bury it. You have to let what God has placed in you out into the world."

You see, this was one of the many exchanges my wife and I have had with each other. In this instance, Chantal began to experience the feelings of quitting something she knew God had put on her heart. The sentiments of unworthiness, rejection, and inadequacy settled in.

As her husband and covering, I could not allow anything to hinder those under my responsibility from becoming all that God has destined for them to become. I have made the decision to fight for her and our children, even if it included coming into direct conflict *with* them about it.

When it is from the place of love, conflict will always breed growth and strength. When it is from the posture of anger or contempt, it will always produce the destruction of relationships, self-worth, future opportunities, etc.

By the end of our argument, Chantal hugged me again and gave me one of those intimate kisses that said, "Thank you for not stopping." It is moments like this where I realized that my heart wasn't to make her become someone new but to help her understand who she already was. In essence, my plan was to reintroduce my wife to the powerful Chantal that was dormant inside of her. I wanted to reintroduce her to "her."

Two Reintroductions

As our King Jesus walked the earth, many would say that He came to reintroduce Man to God. That fact is correct as there had not been a prophetic voice from God for close to 400 years (time difference between Malachi and Matthew). But, as we peer into the Gospels, Jesus also planned to do one more reintroduction. He wanted to reintroduce Man to himself. He knew the power endued on Man from the beginning of time and desired to show them.

Jesus contained this conviction so deep within His heart that He consistently pushed His disciples to go outside of their comfort zone. Heck, He even did not plan to rescue them when they were on a boat about to drown!

In Mark's account of Jesus walking on water, it does not include Peter walking on the water, but it does include a specific sentence that is noteworthy to consider. When I noticed it and dug into the true meaning, it radically changed my view of myself and Jesus at the ultimate Empowerer. Let's look at the story together so you can view yourself in a greater light as well!

> Then He saw them straining at rowing, for the wind was against them. Now about the fourth watch of the night He came to them, walking on the sea, and **would have passed them by**. And when they saw Him walking on the sea, they supposed it was a ghost, and cried out; for they all saw Him and were troubled. But immediately He talked with them and said to them, "Be of good cheer! It is I; do not be afraid." (Mark 6:48-50, NKJV)

As the disciples were trying to get to the destination given by Jesus, they began to face immense resistance. The wind opposed them forcefully and caused the waves to rise up in addition. It seemed nearly impossible to get to Bethesda because of what they faced, but they did have the Son of God in their corner. He has helped them many times before and would surely do it again. This time would be no different, right?

Yes, that's right! This time would be no different. But before we rush to conclusions, we need to change our paradigms about Jesus' intentions with them and with us. You see, the first time Jesus was in a storm with His disciples (Mark 4:35-41), He was infuriated that they woke Him up from a nap due to their fear of drowning. He helped them the first time, but it wasn't His original intention. Jesus would have gladly stayed asleep, knowing the Father would not allow them to perish.

The second time around, Jesus was going to do the same thing again. He was not planning on rescuing them from the storm and it was for one specific reason that is not mentioned much but needs to be shared with you; it is the same reason He would have gladly stayed asleep the first time. Check out verse 48 again.

> Then He saw them straining at rowing, for the wind was against them. Now about the fourth watch of the night He came to them, walking on the sea, and **would have passed them by**. (Mark 6:48, NKJV)

When you look at the word "would" in the phrase "would have passed them by" in the Greek it is the word *thelō* which means "being fully determined and purposed to do." In other words, Jesus was fully determined and made it a purpose in His heart to pass them by. He did not plan to help them with the wind and waves. What caused Jesus to not desire to rescue His disciples? What influenced Him to such a degree that He did not plan on stopping for them? Let's read verses 51 to 52 to find out.

> Then He went up into the boat to them, and the wind ceased. And they were greatly amazed in themselves beyond measure, and marveled. **For they had not understood about the loaves**, because their heart was hardened. (Mark 6:51-52, NKJV)

The last verse is very intriguing because their awe about themselves, and their hearts being hardened from understanding what Jesus communicated to them about the loaves. But what does bread have to do with Jesus not intending to save them? And if them being marveled in themselves and in Jesus had everything to do with this lesson, then what principle was He attempting to teach them that could be so important? Luckily for us, we only have to travel one story up to discover the lesson Jesus tried to teach His disciples and us today.

In Mark 6:33-34, Jesus is teaching the multitudes right after the Twelve return from being sent out to do miracles, heal the sick, cast out demons, and preach the Kingdom. They are on this mission trip level spiritual high - if you've ever been on one, you know what I'm talking about - and are divulging everything to their Rabbi (v. 30) before the crowds assemble.

After hours of teaching, the disciples – who had just come from their action-packed trip – are imploring Jesus to send everyone away so they can eat to avoid intense hunger. This is the moment the Rabbi looks at His disciples and says,

> But He answered and said to them, "**You** give them something to eat." (Mark 6:37a, NKJV)

This was their opportunity to continue to operate with the power and authority that had been placed on them before.

After all, they had just casted demons out and healed the sick, so how hard could multiplying a meal be?

> And they said to Him, "**Shall we go and buy two hundred denarii worth of bread** and give them something to eat?" (Mark 6:37b, NKJV)

So instead of the disciples operating with the mindset of authority and power they recently experienced, they chose to slip back into limiting terms and mindsets. They began to do earthly math instead of choosing to access Heavenly authority. It is because of how fast they forgot their authority that Jesus takes over.

> But He said to them, "How many loaves do you have? Go and see." And when they found out they said, "Five, and two fish."... And when He had taken the five loaves and the two fish, He looked up to heaven, blessed and broke the loaves, and gave them to His disciples to set before them; and the two fish He divided among them all. (Mark 6:38, 41, NKJV)

As He gets everyone to sit down, Jesus blessed the bread and divided it into the disciples' basket to pass out. And this is the moment where the miracle happens, but it comes from an unlikely source.

> So they all ate and were filled. And they took up **twelve baskets full** of fragments and of the fish. Now those who

had eaten the loaves were about five thousand
men. (Mark 6:42-44, NKJV)

When Jesus originally divided the bread and fish in
the disciples' baskets, it hadn't multiplied yet. If it multiplied
enough to feed five thousand men – not counting women and
children – then the baskets wouldn't have been big enough to
carry them to pass it out, especially noting the fact that they
had too many leftovers afterwards!

The miracle of the multiplication of the bread never
happened in the hands of Jesus; it occurred in the hands of the
disciples when they were passing it out. In other words, when
Jesus told them, 'You feed them', *He meant it*. He knew that
they were going to perform the miracle no matter what,
whether He had to give them a small nudge in the form of a
request or a big push in the form of initiating the first step in
the process. And that is the beauty of our King! He goes to
great lengths to show us the supernatural power and divine
potential that is laid dormant within all of us.

The lesson of the loaves that the disciples did not
understand was that they were powerful enough to feed those
people themselves. They had already been endued with

supernatural power and authority from Heaven to perform miracles prior, and Jesus wanted them to continue in that mindset.

He didn't want their revival to be event that lasted only for a moment; He wanted it to become an identity that lasted a lifetime. He purposely set them up by sending them out two-by-two to do miracles, pushed them to feed the five thousand, and did not intend to save them from the storm because they were already powerful enough to deal with it themselves.

Jesus wasn't walking on the earth to only show His power; He was also here to show us our power. This is why He chose to model what a man or woman's life could look like if he or she fully surrendered to the Holy Spirit and made the Gospel of the Kingdom his or her focus.

Your thoughts, words, and actions are more powerful than you were initially told. You are not ordinary, powerless, or normal. You are unique, powerful, and supernatural. Your words have the power to create life and death (Proverbs 18:21), move mountains (Matthew 17:20), and stop the rain (James 5:17-18).

Rejecting the Cheap Versions of Ourselves

Satan's ploy during this time is to gain access to your power and delegated rulership by making you see yourself as less than you are. If you see yourself as a victim instead of more than a conqueror, then you'll never rise up to resist him. This is the exact same temptation brought to Eve and Jesus. When the devil talks to Eve about not eating from the fruit, he says this,

> Then the serpent said to the woman, "You will not surely die. For God knows that in the day you eat of it your eyes will be opened, and **you will be like God**, knowing good and evil." (Genesis 3:4-5, NKJV)

This statement from Satan in the form of a serpent was an attack on their identity. He was devaluing them before their own eyes, and they were too ignorant or naïve to notice. The devaluation is found in the words "you will be like God."

The primary problem with this is that they already were like God. The Creator literally formed them out of His own image and seed! After successfully making Adam and Eve fall in the Garden with that scheme, he tries to use it later on with Jesus.

> And the devil said to Him, "**IF** You are the Son of God, command this stone to become bread." (Luke 4:3, NKJV, emphasis mine)

The phrase "If you are the Son of God" is woven all throughout Satan's language during his temptation of Christ in the wilderness. He knew that if he deceived the first Adam and Eve with the devaluation of their identity, then he can possibly use the same trick to deceive the last Adam to fall. But it did not work because Jesus was well aware of who He was.

Since Satan was unsuccessful with the last Adam, he has now shifted his attention towards attacking the identity of His bride, the Church. If he can get the sons and daughters of God to see themselves as less than they really are, then he can confidently declare, "checkmate!"

You and I are in this battle against our enemy, but we are not unaware of his schemes and plots. You can say the Bride of Christ is the last Eve, the life-giving spirit that came from the last Adam, born out of His side being pierced and now the life that we can give to the world was initially contained in Him. Apart from His piercings and scars, we would have no life, just as Eve did not have life apart from God molding her from Adam's rib.

Since the pictures reflect substantially all throughout the Scriptures about our power and rulership as the Bride of Christ, Satan's ploy is to sell us on a cheap version of who we really are. We cannot buy the discounted version he offers us when God already paid full price for us. It is time we took our rightful place in the world and stopped living on a lower level we were not created for.

You are:

- Royalty (1 Pet. 2:9)
- King or queen (Rev. 1:6)
- A priest or priestess (Rev. 1:6)
- Seated in heavenly places (Eph. 2:6)
- Affirmed and approved of
- Loved with the same love the Father loved Jesus with (John 17:26)
- Powerful beyond measure
- Assigned to be served by angels (Heb. 1:14)

- Filled with the fullness of God (Eph. 3:19)
- Given the entire Kingdom as a gift (Luke 12:32)
- A representative of Heaven (2 Cor. 5:20)
- Freely given everything that's of lesser value than Christ (Rom. 8:32)
- Someone with enough authority in the spiritual realm to judge angels and instruct them (1 Cor. 6:3; Eph. 3:10)
- And so much more.

All of what's listed above is who you are as a child of the King, not what your circumstances, people, Satan, or yourself has said about you.

You are not:

- Stupid
- Ugly
- Meaningless
- Powerless
- Alone
- Neglected
- Mediocre

- Unloved
- A failure
- "Too much"
- A victim
- A peasant or slave
- And anything else that puts you down

It's time you began to realize the throne God has you sitting on, the crown He's placed on your head, and the scepter He's placed in your hands. You have been given dominion and power to expand His Kingdom, first in your home and then in our world. As you take responsibility for your world and partner with the Holy Spirit to change it to reflect Heaven, you'll discover the authority that's been implanted in you as God's image-bearer on the earth.

Your family will become more loving, your finances will be healed, your impact will increase, miracles will become more commonplace, your bond with God will deepen, and His joy will permeate your heart. You will no longer agree with the beliefs or lies that come in your head. You will recognize what is the whisper of the enemy instead of the whisper of God and will forcefully take it captive to obey Christ (2 Corinthians 10:5).

Nothing in the earthly realm or the spiritual realm was created to stop you, except God Himself. Today is the day you start to believe your authority and take up the mantle of the Kingdom to change this world and make it look like the country we are from. No demon can defeat you, no power in Hell can hinder you, no attack too great you cannot overcome, no obstacle too strong you cannot endure with joy and clarity, no challenge too unique you cannot solve it, and no responsibility too big you cannot bear with the strength of Christ.

Our ancestors were kings and queens in Eden. It is about time we embraced that we are too. You and I are not powerless beings; we were born to rule. Now that we have reclaimed this all-important reality, let's go forward and see what embracing this will mean for our churches, our world, and our lives.

Key Principles

1. Jesus not only came to reintroduce Man to God, but to also reintroduce Man to himself.

2. The bread to feed the multitudes did not multiply in the hands of Jesus, but in the hands of the disciples when they were passing it out.

3. God does not want revival to last for a moment, but for it to become an identity that lasts a lifetime.

4. Jesus did not intend to save His disciples from the storm because they were already powerful enough to deal with it themselves.

5. Satan's ploy is to sell us on a cheap version of who we really are. Do not settle for that discounted version when God paid full price for us.

6. You are royalty, a king or queen, seated in heavenly places, powerful beyond measure, assigned to be served by angels, filled with the fullness of God, given the entire Kingdom as a gift, freely given everything that's of lesser value than Christ and someone with enough authority in the spiritual

realm to judge angels and instruct them.

7.   Nothing in the earthly realm or the spiritual realm was created to stop you, except God Himself.

8.   There is no demon that can defeat you, no power in Hell that can hinder you, no attack too great you cannot overcome, no obstacle too strong you cannot endure with joy and clarity, no challenge too unique you cannot solve it, and no responsibility too big you cannot bear with the strength of Christ.

What Will This Mean for Our Churches?

All throughout the Bible, whenever God wanted to create a meaningful change in the world, He first began with His own house, with His own people. Before He ever judged any other nation or enacted positive transformation, He first brought it to His children.

This is because God is the perfect Judge and the greatest Father – He will never expect the world to live by the standards He does not set for His house first. God is perfectly righteous because He will not act as a hypocrite, which is someone who advises people to do something they themselves or the ones closest to them will not abide by.

Because of His perfect fatherhood nature, when the rulership identity hidden inside of every believer is realized and uncovered, it will first affect the Church before it changes the world. The work and transformation will begin in-house before it gets taken out. The disposition and nature of the children of God will be altered drastically that within the next ten years, we will not look the same.

We will shine brighter, be emotionally stronger, mentally sharper, spiritually connected, and socially responsible. All of these dramatic changes will end up spilling out into every fabric of society and every arena of influence because these effects were never meant to stay inside the four walls of a building simply because we were always meant to be "called out ones" (Greek word for church is ecclesia which means "called out ones" in simplest terms).

The Rulership Effect in Our Churches

Make no mistake, before the world gets touched by God, His Body gets touched by Him. He will not ignore the needs of His children before caring for the needs of the world because He meant for His family to be the catalysts for every significant change on earth. As I have prayed, pastored, counseled hundreds of people, and preached to thousands at once, I sense there are five incredible shifts that will take place in the Body when our rulership identity is embraced and actualized.

1. More ***empowered*** believers
2. More ***powerful*** Children of God
3. More ***influential*** Christians
4. More ***secure*** saints
5. More ***responsible*** representatives

More Empowered Believers

One of the preliminary effects that discovering our rulership identity will have in the Church will be developing more empowered believers. As someone who has been involved in ministry either full-time or part-time since the age of 19, the shift towards the ministering or impacting people to be done by the many instead of by the few is one that I know will alter the entire landscape of the family of God.

This will come as a result of every believer realizing they are anointed in their own right. We will all understand that since we have been baptized into one Body (1 Corinthians 12:13), then we are all a part of the Body of the Messiah, which means "Anointed One", and therefore, are all heavily anointed as a result.

We will move into greater partnerships with the pastors or overseers of our churches to honor their anointing to preach and lead a church, while adding our own personal anointing to create wealth, restore marriages, think strategically, provide prophetic insights, or pray for people to be healed supernaturally.

We will no longer settle for ministry being done solely by those in positional authority but will welcome it being done by those in Kingdom authority. This means more believers will be developed, empowered, and released to bring their strength, skills, and spirit to the table to impact people.

This reminds me of when I was given the opportunity to speak to our church for three minutes on a Saturday outdoor in-person prayer gathering. I was tasked with encouraging them during the pandemic about never giving up hope and then praying at the end to dismiss our prayer gathering. What was interesting was how I used those three minutes.

For one minute, I told them (rather quickly, I would add) that God created each of them kings and queens under Him. For the last two minutes, I empowered them to take this knowledge from their minds to their hearts, not believe for one moment that the devil can defeat you in any circumstance if you have Christ in you, and gave them one thing to do to apply it practically to their lives.

The last thing that came out of my mouth as I transitioned into praying for them to go forward shocked me as it came out of my mouth.

"Now, as I transition into praying to end this gathering, I want you to know what I'm *not* going to pray for. I'm not going to pray for everything to go away or for things to get better. What I *will* pray is for your eyes to be opened to the king or queen that is already inside of you because when your eyes are opened to who you really are, you will be able to partner with Jesus to conquer what you are currently facing and defeat the devil."

As those words left my mouth, I could see some people's eyes open wide in shock and others be filled with tears. I then prayed for their eyes to be opened and for them to be strengthened by Jesus in the inner man through the Holy

Spirit. A few hours after the gathering, Chantal and I received text messages from many people thanking us for empowering them. There was one text message in particular that Chantal received that struck me:

> *Good morning, friend. I just wanted to say thank you so much for what you and your husband are doing, equipping the church like never before to realize the power of the kingdom that we have inside of us. That's when changes will really happen. Thank you so much and God bless you both.*

Even though I was taking a massive risk uttering those words out of my mouth as a pastor, I understood that people more than ever love being empowered. It further cemented the reality that this aligns with our God-given nature more than any other thing because our design is one of delegated authority and empowerment from the Creator anyways.

This personally brought more freedom to my soul than I knew I needed because it released me from the bondage of always being needed. Being in vocational ministry, it was almost an unspoken norm for you to be needed all of the time and sacrifices had to be made in order to properly meet the needs of the people you are pastoring. Gratefully, that is not the truth. I can now prioritize my marriage, family, and personal health without losing impact simply because people now understood they were rulers and could take dominion themselves.

We will have more pastors with vibrant marriages, healthy homes, strong mental and emotional health, joyful dispositions, and creative investment in the things they enjoy. Less pastors would drop out within three years and burnout will become an afterthought instead of a norm. People will take more risks and solve problems while telling our pastors, "It's okay. You can rest on this problem. I will take care of this one for you. Enjoy your family day and I will call you tomorrow with how I figured it out."

More Powerful Children of God

As the Church, we have been adopted by Almighty God to be His children (John 1:12-13) and endued with power through the Holy Spirit (Acts 1:8). The position in the family of God is a privilege none of us deserve, but once we are in the family and our rulership identity is accepted, false humility will be rejected, and we will fully embrace the greatness He's placed inside each of us through His Kingdom.

Our hearts will then be filled with the love of God to such a measure that we cannot help but pour everything we have for the sake of others. The atmosphere of our gatherings will be a place of tangible love and power through messages backed with fire, prayers saturated with the Holy Spirit, spiritual gifts on full display, and personal encouragements that eternally mark people.

The default mode will be giving rather than receiving because our hearts will be coming from a place of abundance instead of a place of lack. When we give generously like this in any way, it means we are whole and secure emotionally – that is, if we give with a cheerful heart.

When we operate out of a place of abundance and wholeness, it becomes nearly inevitable for us to realize that we are powerful. And this is what will happen to the Church around the world. The Sons and Daughters of Almighty God will see themselves as powerful because they won't always feel like they lack something, they are not 'good enough', or are in some way unworthy to be carrying an anointing.

Every Sunday our gathering will see more demonstrations of the tangible power of God because we come into the assembly with an expectation to give to others through the spiritual gifts given by the Holy Spirit.

It will display the very atmosphere of Heaven here on earth because it reflects our Father who is the Ultimate Giver – He loved us so much that He gave His only Son (John 3:16). And as you know, being in a relationship with a giver is far more uplifting than being in one with a taker and the children of God will all make this shift together to be the greatest givers the world has ever seen.

When we realize we were born to rule under Christ, then the demonstration of the Holy Spirit's tangible power will be displayed more often because people will be more focused on how they can serve each other in their gifts of edification, leadership, communication, shepherding, mercy, prophecy, healing, etc. How powerful would we become if we focused more on giving than receiving?

For you personally, as wholeness enters your heart through the love and power of God, your mind will change from receiving to giving because you have the fullness of God inside of you. You will begin praying for more miracles with authority, believing for bigger things for others, loving with no reservations, and giving as if you already have it all.

When the children of God adopt this attitude, there would be no limit to what we can do or what we can become. The impact the Body of Christ would have on their respective nations would be unprecedented. No number of setbacks, obstacles, resistance, success, money, place, platforms or possessions would hinder the Kingdom of God advancing into the world.

More Influential Christians

When Christians are genuinely empowered and adopt the mindset that they are powerful, then what proceeds, as a result, is that we have more influential Christians. No longer will we allow ourselves to settle for our Christian lives to be defined by one day of the week, our Bible knowledge, and our friendly personalities.

As a result, there will no longer be attempts to kill any type of ambition or a desire for success and influence due to previous associations of labeling those desires as evil. We will step out to lead culture and impact the world, not to avoid it or reject it completely. The culture and the world will no longer in its essence be regarded as wholly evil, only its *patterns* will be seen as that (Romans 12:2).

The beautiful thing about our King's desire for the Church was for Her to be designed by Him to produce so much power and wisdom that Her influence would supersede the culture of the physical world to impact the spiritual realm! Read what Paul says in Ephesians 3,

> And to make all see what is the fellowship of the mystery, which from the beginning of the ages has been hidden in God who created all things through Jesus Christ; **to the intent that now the manifold wisdom of God might be made known by the church to the principalities and powers in the heavenly places,** according to the eternal purpose which He accomplished in Christ Jesus our Lord (Ephesians 3:9-11, NKJV)

It is evident that one of the reasons God set up the Church through Christ was to be so influential that we would impact spiritual principalities. And if you read Genesis, then you know the spiritual realm preceded the physical realm (Genesis 1:1). This reveals that the spiritual is more potent than the physical and has a more significant effect.

Therefore, if one of the purposes of the Church is to radically impact the more powerful realm, then this shift in our identity will embolden Christians to no longer shy away from influencing the lesser realm. After all, we are called to bring Heaven to earth, not just sit around and wait for earth to go bad.

More Secure Saints

If you ever want to impact and shape the values or beliefs of a nation, hit their educational system, so you can influence the future politicians and lawmakers while they are young. The reason young children are targeted heavily is because they are more impressionable due to their belief systems being established during their younger adolescent years.

Because children have this in their nature and desire to follow the examples of strong adult leadership, they will take their teachings and belief systems to heart for themselves. This is how the moral decay of a country begins. It didn't start with the results of the previous election.

It started with a transformation of the educational system twenty years prior. If children can be greatly influenced by what is taught by adults, how much more will spiritually born-again Christians be influenced by the teachings of mature, adult Christians, especially when teachings on our rulership identity will ring out all throughout every platform, altar, and church across the globe?

It will be a beautiful sight to behold and a wonder to experience as the Church births and develops more secure saints. The kind of home we will become will be one that produces children who no longer see themselves as servants or slaves needing to pay a debt or "make up the difference" by being as good as possible for their Father. They will view themselves not as a peasant in the field, but a child in the palace. This environment will produce sons and daughters that are grateful for their adoption into this royal family and no longer fear judgment from their Dad.

Make no mistake, we all have sinned and fallen short of the glory of God (Romans 3:23) and need His Grace to save us. Without God's initiation, we cannot ever experience the power of His love, approval, peace, joy, etc.

But the reality and truth of the Scriptures that will be proclaimed is that after you make the choice to follow Jesus, you are adopted into the family and restored back to your position of rulership. We are to no longer regard ourselves as sinners but as *saints*. Even one of the greatest verses that proclaims us being sinners will be redeemed for what Paul was truly trying to communicate,

> But God demonstrates His own love toward us, in that **while we were** still sinners, Christ died for us. (Romans 8:12, NKJV)

The three words in that verse which makes all of the difference are: "while we were". In other words, when we *were* sinners, Christ died for us. This means the identity of "sinner" is intended to be a past-tense identity description of us. Paul even communicates this reality when he addresses those same Roman Christians in his opening remarks of the epistle,

What Will This Mean for Our Churches?

> To all who are in Rome, beloved of God, called to be
> **saints**: Grace to you and peace from God our Father and
> the Lord Jesus Christ. (Romans 1:7, NKJV)

It is as plain as can be there. They were called to be
saints, and we are, too. How much brighter would the Church
shine when She hears from Her pulpits to hide Her light?
How much more secure would Christians be if they were told
they were saints instead of sinners? Now, this does not mean
we never sin or rarely struggle with temptation. Still, it does
mean our identity will be established in a place of holiness and
royalty (saints) over a place of sinfulness and worthlessness
(sinners).

Our churches will be more holy and righteous because
we will not accept an identity that still connects us to sin. The
truth is that it is much easier to resist sin and temptation when
you don't even identify with it.

It is like the time when I stopped playing baseball after
one year of Tee-ball because I did not identify myself as a
baseball player. This caused a lot of pain in my family because
I was the only Santiago in my lineage to not enjoy baseball, but
since I did not identify myself with it, I did not actively

participate in it. In the Church, we will have more born-again saints, not born-again sinners and it will be a beauty to behold.

More Responsible Representatives

As our collective identity as the Body of Christ elevates to match that of the rulership identity we have been given, then our sense of responsibility for our neighborhoods, cities, regions, and countries will grow.

Because we have been delegated authority to disciple all the nations, we would have bigger questions like: What would we need to do to disciple the entire nation of America, Brazil, Italy, or Australia? What kind of initiatives and partnerships would we need to create if we are going to baptize the entire nation of America on one day in the name of the Father, Son and the Holy Spirit?

With this transformed mindset, our hearts would enlarge and would reflect our Father's heart better because we would feel the duty to make every area of society where we are planted to look like Heaven. Since we have been given the earth to steward and a mandate to transform culture to reflect Him, our obligation to change neighborhoods, build up homes, step into positions of influence, start great businesses, aid the marginalized, and free the oppressed would massively increase.

Where the people of God reside will change to no longer struggle with fatherlessness, poverty, crime, low self-worth, corruption in business or politics, or people disconnected from our King all because made the decision and said to the devil, "This is our region, not yours anymore. Because we are here, we have taken personal responsibility and now it's time for you to go. This place is ours now." Our effects on where we live would match that of what God spoke through the prophet Jeremiah to His people who were in exile in Babylon,

> Also, seek the **peace** and **prosperity** of the **city** to which I have carried you into exile. Pray to the Lord for it, because if it prospers, you too will prosper. (Jeremiah 29:7, NIV)

The day is coming and is near as the Bride of Christ will embrace a new mindset when it comes to "being the hands and feet of Jesus". The description will now include being a literal representative of the King of Kings, the One who is royal, holy, powerful, mighty, influential, wise, strong, anointed, wealthy, supernatural, sacrificial, and loving. All that He is will be all that we will become here on earth as we take on His name and spread it to the world.

Key Principles

1. Whenever God wants to do a meaningful change in the world, He first begins with His own house, with His own people.

2. God is the perfect Judge and greatest Father - He will never expect the world to live by the standards He does not set for His house first.

3. Every believer is heavily anointed in their own right.

4. The empowerment of believers will translate to ministry being done by the many, not the few and by those in Kingdom authority instead of those in positional authority.

5. When we operate out of a place of abundance and wholeness, it becomes nearly inevitable for us to realize that we are powerful.

6. Our Father who is the Ultimate Giver – He loved us so much that He gave His Son.

7. As wholeness enters your heart through the love and power of God, your mind will change from receiving to giving

because you have the fullness of God inside of you.

8. The Church was designed by our King to produce so much power and wisdom that Her influence would supersede the culture of the physical world to impact the spiritual realm.

9. We are called to bring Heaven to earth, not just sit around and wait for earth to go bad.

10. It is much easier to resist sin and temptation when you don't even identify with it.

11. When the people of God take personal responsibility over the condition of their regions, it won't be long before the devil has to flee that region.

What Will This Mean for Our World?

As the Bride of Christ embraces the hand of Jesus for the purpose of rulership, we will experience a Church whose influence will no longer be limited to a building or a day of the week. This will come because of a simple, yet profound truth that just as Adam and Eve were designed to rule their world to make it look like Heaven, so the last Adam and His Bride – the Church – are called to create a massive worldwide impact that will make the earth reflect the homeland of Heaven. The rulership mandate did not change from Genesis with Man entrusted with dominion to Revelation with Christ establishing His Kingdom in its entirety.

The Rulership Effect in Our World

When the Church shifts Her view from waiting to live in eternity to training for rulership in eternity, then it will not be long for the world to be transformed before eternity. We will become the catalysts we were always meant to become and will partner with our Father to bring significant change to a dark and hopeless world. Having several conversations with former mayors, wealthy business owners, people who administer aid to single mothers and the homeless, and spending endless amounts of time in prayer, I sense there are four monumental effects that will take place in the world after our King has used our rulership identity to revitalize His Church.

1. Improved *societal* conditions
2. National leaders with *integrity*
3. Nations will be *saved*
4. The world will get *better*, not worse

Improved Societal Conditions

One of the primary effects that discovering our rulership identity will have on the world will be experiencing the improvement of every area of society. When the family of God takes personal responsibility for the state of the earth we have been entrusted with by our Father (Psalm 115:16), we will not stand by and watch will our world deteriorates day-by-day, year-by-year. We will get involved in a major way, seeking to unite across denominational lines solely for one mission: bringing Heaven to our city, region, and nation.

It will spill out to the neighborhoods, prisons, families, economic systems, education systems, businesses, and positions of power. People will lay down their minor quarrels with each other and properly assess the major needs of where they live. They will create a battle plan on how to improve the rates at which fathers stay at home and, as a result, reduce crime, illiteracy and poverty rates. Restoring the family dynamics and the father back to the home is of such chief importance in the eyes of God that the last verse of the Old Testament reads like this,

> Behold, I will send you Elijah the prophet before the great and awesome day of the Lord comes. And he will turn the hearts of **fathers** to their **children** and the hearts of **children** to their **fathers**, lest I come and strike the **land** with a decree of **utter destruction**. (Malachi 4:5-6, NKJV)

God directly correlates with the land being struck with destruction to the lack of the restoration of the father to the children. He intimately knows the devastation that can take place when the father is not in connection with his children. After all, when Adam rebelled against God, it was a son rebelling against his Father. The world experienced dire consequences due to his decision.

It is the same with our current world. The conditions of our world have been deteriorating more and more because of the estrangement of strong men leading their homes. Many of us have experienced some type of wound from our fathers or male authority figures so we intimately know the pain that can cause. This is why when the Bride of Christ takes responsibility for this world, She will rise up to first restore the father back to the family because the issues in society are first solved by restoring the family dynamic and second lifting up the community.

The Church will then begin to look at healing the other needs our world has like abortion, racism, homelessness, hunger, and healthy reintegration of inmates back into society. We will no longer separate each underlying issue according to specific political parties nor allow ourselves to get divided by the news the outside world is providing.

We will care about ending abortion, but simultaneously improving our adoption and foster care system to assist those babies and mothers who did not get an abortion. We will care about ending racism and police brutality, while simultaneously protecting our police and military because all of these are all the right thing to do. We will no longer pick and choose based on two parties but will make decisions together based on one Kingdom. This Kingdom we are a part of wants to make *all* of earth to look like Heaven, not just some areas of it.

Our unification will speak volumes to the world that many will flock to the Church because of how we love each other and how deeply we care about our neighborhoods and cities. Each person within the family of God will not have a heart for every issue, but they will have a heart for some issue and will be willing to partner with their brothers and sisters to move forward in changing the very landscape of where they reside. Every local church will not take the role of improving every area of society but will take responsibility for improving their area that they have been assigned by God.

National Leaders with Integrity

One of the many prevalent issues in the world are leaders who are either political or business leaders who lack integrity. They are ones who wink with their eyes, smooth in their talk, but devise evil in their heart (Proverbs 6:12-14). The unfortunate reality is that many leaders in the world who influence their respective nations do not operate with the integrity necessary to bring about widespread blessings.

But all of this will change when the children of God embrace the rulership identity that is their birthright. In the next coming years, I sense a huge shift for believers and pastors to not shy away from the arenas of business and politics. This will be because our mindset will change from a church mindset to a kingdom mindset. What is the difference between those two? There are multiple, but there are three prevalent contrasts that will directly affect the leadership of nations.

1. A church mindset is focused on God's rule through pastors, bishops, and deacons **over those in a church congregation**; a kingdom mindset is focused on God's rule **over every nation and the entire created order**.

2. A church mindset views the Bible as a **religious book** that helps us escape the world and get to Heaven; a kingdom mindset views the Bible **as a blueprint** that can disciple a whole nation and create structure in every aspect of society.

3. A church mindset **isolates** the Gospel from economics, politics, and public policy; a kingdom mindset **integrates** the Gospel into the economics, politics, and public policy of their regions and nations.

As our collective mindset makes this drastic shift, more Jesus-centered billionaire business owners and politicians will rise up. The Church will champion those who feel the destiny to run for office or become an ultra-wealthy CEO and will no longer shy away from speaking about the topics of money or politics from Her pulpits.

We will experience more Christians stepping into positions of influence all over the world and there will be less corruption at the top since there will be leaders with integrity occupying them. Less corruption equals better transparency and honesty which results in everyone being blessed because of it.

Nations Will Be Saved

The King we love and serve is not satisfied with society improving or national leaders with integrity if whole nations do not submit to His Lordship. Before His ascension, Jesus commanded His disciples to "make disciples of all the nations" (Matt. 28:19a, NASB) and baptize them into the name of the Father, the Son, and the Holy Spirit (v. 19b).

Many of His disciples were simple fishermen who were used to a life of mediocrity, not one of large influence, and yet our Lord gave His kingly commission for them to take all the nations and baptize them into His name. He would give them His authority, His name, and the Holy Spirit to accomplish this task.

The Great Commission is really a call for the Church to partner in the family business of making this earth like Heaven. It is a prompting for us to operate as co-heirs with Christ and receive His inheritance. What is His inheritance? It is the nations of the world.

> I will declare the decree: The Lord has said to Me, 'You are My Son, today I have begotten You. Ask of Me, and I will give You **the nations for Your inheritance**, and the

ends of the earth for Your possession. (Psalm 2:7-8, NKJV)

More than ever, Christians today are having their eyes opened by the Holy Spirit about this inheritance and are giving up their lives to see this occur. Even non-profits and initiatives have been created for this sole purpose. Chantal and I have been able to partner with a non-profit named Missions.Me that runs this initiative called 1Nation1Day. The heart behind this initiative is asking the question, "Can a nation be saved in a day?"

They have successfully been able to perform this initiative in Honduras, the Dominican Republic, Nicaragua, and Peru. It has been so life-transforming in multiple ways. First, I met my wife on the trip to the Dominican Republic. Second, it is awe-inspiring to be a part of group that possesses favor with entire governments and are given access to impact schools with the Gospel, perform business conferences with their people, supply shoes to thousands of children, provide free medical attention to their people, build water filters for towns, perform radio interviews, and be given access to send text messages to everyone in their country to attend their local stadium event where millions of people across the country surrender their lives to Jesus at one time. And all of these things are done in the span of one week with tens of thousands of Christians coming in from multiple countries around the world.

As the Body of Christ step into positions of influence, create businesses that supply billions of dollars while increasing the quality of life for people, and take responsibility for the needs of their region, it will not be long before we get to see entire nations saved.

Stadiums will be over capacity with hungry souls, fields will be filled with repentant hearts, and whole bodies of water will be used for mass baptisms. Those moments will feed our souls and cause us to be even more grateful for our King and His Kingdom, as they have done for me and my wife.

The World Will Get Better, Not Worse

When the issues in our society improve, leadership positions in national offices and influential companies are filled with people of integrity, and whole nations are saved, what ultimately follows is the condition of the world getting better, not worse.

What may shock many people, including myself a few months before this writing, is that if the Church is focused on fulfilling the line in our King's prayer, "Your kingdom come Your will be done on earth as it is in heaven" (Matthew 6:10), then our worldview should be one of excitement than doom and gloom.

If you think about it in the simplest way, if the earth is changing to begin looking like Heaven, then diseases should diminish, poverty should become a rarity, persecution should lessen, whole nations should be saved, crime should be minimized, and the list goes on. Since Heaven is our focus and our blueprint, light will increase in the world and overtake darkness.

People will be set free from addiction, marriages will be restored, racism will be eradicated, and the name of Jesus will be revered everywhere. The end-time view of our world and the return of our King would match that of the historical context of when He prayed this prayer.

When He returns to the colony of earth a second time, He should expect it to be a beautiful reflection of the homeland of Heaven in the same way Caesar expected every colony to be an exact replica of the homeland of Rome.

Because of this worldview shift and the effects that will occur, we will see more Christians not shrinking back from running after the dreams God has placed on their hearts, saying 'yes' to getting married and raising their children to be giant slayers, impacting the younger generations, and restoring the others ones who have lost their way. Millions will submit their lives to the Lordship of King Jesus and our world will be in better hands as the transfer of wealth and power will go from the hands of the wicked to the righteous.

That will be such a powerful movement to be a part of. The only question I have is: will you be an active participant of it, or will you sit on the sidelines?

Key Principles

1. Just as Adam and Eve were designed to rule their world to make it look like Heaven, so the last Adam and His Bride – the Church – are called to create a massive worldwide impact that will make the earth reflect the homeland of Heaven.

2. The rulership mandate has not changed from Genesis with Man being given dominion to Revelation with Christ establishing His Kingdom in its entirety.

3. When the family of God takes personal responsibility for the state of the earth we have been entrusted with by our Father, we will not stand by and watch will our world deteriorates day-by-day, year-by-year.

4. One of the main issues the Church must focus on restoring is the reintegration of strong men into the family household. God directly correlates the condition of the world to the father being disconnected from his family.

5. The Kingdom we are a part of wants to make all of earth look like Heaven, not just parts of it.

6. There will be a huge shift coming for believers and pastors to not shy away from the arenas of business and politics.

7. When there are righteous people in positions of power, transparency and honesty occurs which results in widespread blessing for all who are affected.

8. Our King is not satisfied until all the nations submit under His Lordship.

9. The Great Commission is a call for the Church to partner in the family business of making this earth like Heaven.

10. As the Body of Christ step into positions of influence, create businesses that supply billions of dollars while increasing the quality of life for people, and take responsibility for the needs of their region, it will not be long before we get to see entire nations saved.

11. Since Heaven is our focus and our blueprint, light should increase in the world and overtake darkness.

What Will This Mean for You?

If the Church undergoes a radical transformation and the world follows Her example, then you can be sure that you are included in that process. In fact, I would dare to say that you might be transformed at the same time as the Church, if not before. Since the Church is the people, then the collective body of believers are not changed until the individual believer is changed. This means that your transformation can be a catalyst for the change in our world. And once you are transformed, your family, friends, coworkers, and neighbors will be changed as a result of your presence.

The Rulership Effect in You

When you make the commitment to reclaim your God-given birthright to rule on earth, then every area of your life will be revitalized. Dead dreams will breathe again, good habits will be reinforced, Kingdom relationships will be established, your destiny will be restored, and your future will be brightened. With everything that I could pinpoint as the changes that will occur in your life, I sense that four major enhancements will occur.

1. Revival will become an ***identity***
2. Your authority will be ***actualized***
3. Obstacles will not ***overcome*** you
4. Cutting edge creativity will be ***generated***

Revival Will Become an Identity

The year of 2020 has been one of a major roller coaster. Pandemics, protests, riots, elections, lockdowns, and division has caused everyone to look at the start of the decade with either a grim mindset or one that is aware that something powerful could come as a result of it. Revival has been thrown around in recent years as an event that many people were looking forward to. But in the same year of the coronavirus pandemic, revival became more than a word – it became a reality that seemed closer than ever.

This caused the Church to gather together on beaches, create structures and tents to hold services outdoors, worship with thousands at parks, and express our faith more openly than in years past. Our desire for revival rose up in our hearts so much that many began to look at it in a different light.

Their view of revival shifted from it being an event to it being an identity we take on. It was one with the mindset of: "God does not send revival. He sends His Holy Spirit to fill us and we become revival."

The reality is this: God has already given us everything we need to completely transform this world. He's given us the Holy Spirit, the Word of God, access through prayer, breakthrough through fasting, wisdom and strength through community, and power through His Kingdom. As you take on this rulership message as an identity, what will simultaneously happen will be you taking on revival as an identity. You will no longer regard it as an event for those who are extra holy to lead it but will see it as someone you already are. Revival is not an event waiting to happen, it is an identity waiting to be accepted. This became evident to me when Chantal and I went on a mission trip to Brazil three weeks before lockdowns occurred in the United States.

We were accompanying my alma mater, Southeastern University, to partner with a powerful and influential organization called Dunamis Movement to come alongside their mission to see their entire country of Brazil saved and discipled. The team as a whole had about 100 university students in total, but on our specific team, there were around 27 members, all of them young adults ranging from the ages of 19 to 24.

In the beginning of the trip, when we would go out to the streets and pray for people, I began to notice something interesting. Everyone was timid in their prayers, unsure about who they were or the authority they possessed, and did not see many supernatural events occur. Now I do not measure someone operating in their God-given design by those specific measures, but I knew something was off. This inner knowledge caused me to pull all of them into the only air-conditioned room and share with them the rulership message – one of strength, authority, identity, and supernatural power.

Within a matter of two days, Chantal and I saw a complete transformation in every single one of them. Some of them who would classify themselves as timid before, were now walking up to people with boldness and speaking life into them. A few of them have operated in the spiritual gift of prophecy in the past but were now using that gift with more confidence and accuracy than ever before.

One of them even came up to me after a church service on our second-to-last night and told me, "Christian, I started praying for this one girl and all of a sudden I knew her grandfather was struggling with specific things and that's why she came to this church service. After I started saying what those specific things were, she started crying and told me afterwards, 'That was the most accurate prophetic word I have ever received in my entire life.'"

He attributed his ability to hear the Holy Spirit to the realization that he was powerful, and God wanted to use Him. The newfound knowledge of who he truly was activated his ability to step deeper into a spiritual gift he operated in occasionally. It was actually during that trip that I knew this message needed to get out into the world. God used our time in Brazil to spark what you are now reading with your eyes.

Your identity as a ruler was meant to draw you nearer to God, not do things apart from Him. It was intended for you to walk in relational-rulership with the King of kings and the One that is more powerful than you. So, as you embrace this identity, you will be drawn even deeper into a relationship with the Holy Spirit and revival will become your identity. The supernatural will not be as weird to you, nor seem like that is exclusively for pastors, bishops, deacons, or elders. It will be for you because you are revival.

Your Authority Will Be Actualized

Authority is an interesting word that not a lot of people know what it means. Most of the time it is grouped in with the word power, but it is very different from it. To see plainly what the difference is, consider this analogy: two people have guns so both of them have power, but one of them is an officer with a badge. Which one has the right or authorized to use the power of the gun? The officer. Here's another one: two people would love to see the school system changed and have the power to voice their opinions. One is a mother and the other is the head of the school board. Which one has the right to use their voice and see results? The head of the school board.

Power is not synonymous with authority. The first is defined as the ability to change something, while the second is defined as the right to use that power. If power is expressed without authority, it is seen as illegal or dangerous. In terms of the Kingdom, everyone has power to change things and move things around, but not everyone has been authorized by God to use that power. The difference between a person with power and a person with authority is that the man or woman who possesses authority is someone who has their identity co-signed by God.

Jesus was the perfect example of having His identity co-signed by the Father. After He was baptized by His cousin John, the Father spoke and said, "This is My Son, in whom I am well pleased" (Matthew 3:17). This affirmation and approval caused Jesus to be absolutely secure in who He was that He even told the Pharisees who questioned His authority,

> Jesus answered and said to them, "Even if I bear witness of Myself, My witness is true, for **I know where I came from** and **where I am going**; but you do not know where I come from and where I am going. (John 8:14, NKJV)

His boldness in His identity came from it being co-signed by God. He did not care about proving Himself to anyone nor did He struggle if people's opinions of Him did not match that of His Father. He walked in complete authority and was authorized to use the power implanted inside of Him to heal the sick, multiply bread, raise the dead, restore the blind, make the lame walk, and set the captives free.

This personal sense of authority reminds me of a conversation I had with a Spirit-filled CEO of a multimillion-dollar company at his home. We were sitting in his jacuzzi and talking about his story from being in jail to God taking him to being successful in business. He recounted some of the internal dialogue that occurred with himself as he stepped into rooms with people who were greater than him in business when he first started. He was nervous at first stepping into those rooms, but then God whispered something to him that transformed his outlook.

> "Christian, at first I was nervous, but then God told me, 'If anything happens spiritually either negative or positive, they will not be able to handle it nor lead. Do not be intimidated anymore for you are the spiritual authority in this room."

I remember going silent in that moment because those words pierced my soul. In that moment, the Holy Spirit confirmed the same thing to me. *Christian, stop being intimidated by successful people or those who outwardly have things together. When things are going bad spiritually, you are the spiritual authority I have placed to handle those things.* I have kept that in my heart ever since and have personally seen my ability to take courageous steps increase tremendously.

As you change your view of yourself to match that of the ruler God sees in you, you will also walk with authority. You will no longer be enamored by people who operate in power or have great giftings. You will not see a wide chasm between those who change the room with just their presence and yourself. Confidence and boldness will replace timidity and insecurity. An unshakeable spirit will replace a worried and anxious one.

Obstacles Will Not Overcome You

One of the remarkable changes that occurs inside of a person who embraces their rulership identity is that obstacles no longer overcome them. This does not mean that they will not be affected by them, it just means that obstacles will not subdue them. Feeling hopeless, powerless, or trapped are all byproducts of us encountering a situation that causes us to think there is not a solution. In many of those moments, most of us would react like Adam and Eve when they passed the blame onto everyone or everything else instead of taking responsibility (Adam blamed Eve, Eve blamed the serpent, Genesis 3).

As one makes the journey to change from being a victim to being a ruler, a mindset shift takes place from an external locus of control to an internal locus of control. An external locus of control is simply defined as the reason for the results in your life has everything to do with people, events, and circumstances outside of you. An internal locus of control moves from placing the blame to external factors to accepting the personal responsibility of the results. The dialogue shifts from, "I was late to work because of the traffic" to "I did not check how bad the traffic was ahead of time and so I was unprepared".

Even though it is a simple change, it is definitely not an easy one. However, when one makes the decision to live out the full reality of their birthright to rule, this mindset shift is necessary. It is after this transformation of the mind occurs that you will begin to look at obstacles in a new light. No longer will you see things as impossible because you will be operating at a greater level of faith and a more intimate partnership with the Holy Spirit to overcome what is in front of you. You will realize everything is "figureoutable". Adjusting to new circumstances will be much easier now that you have taken responsibility over the most important factor in the equation: you.

When you take ownership of ruling your mind, heart, and actions, then it will not be long before your outer world reflects the strength, order, joy, peace, and love that you have built up in your inner world. You will genuinely accept the truth James 1:2 where you will count obstacles as pure joy because you know that major breakthrough is on the other side of major conflict. Complaining will lessen because you will accept the truth that the amount of adversity you overcome directly affects the weight of the spiritual authority you possess.

Cutting Edge Creativity Will Be Generated

With the rise of your self-awareness, it will only be a matter of time before you begin creating products, producing films, writing music, starting businesses, publishing books, formulating policies that are ahead of its time. This is because as you realize that the most important word you could ever focus on is access, you will give more access to the Holy Spirit on a daily basis. When the Holy Spirit is given more access through surrender in a believer's life, He always heightens their emotional and mental faculties.

It is through the Holy Spirit that we are given the mind of Christ. It is through the Holy Spirit that the love of God is poured into our hearts. What's noteworthy is that is it also through the Holy Spirit that we can know our future. Yes, you read that correctly.

The Holy Spirit can literally tell you things that are ahead and what God has planned for you. The Father never desired for you to live in darkness over the goodness of His will for your life. He wanted you to know His will for you so much that He gave you His Spirit. If you do not believe me, read 1 Corinthians 2:9-12,

> But as it is written:
> "Eye has not seen, nor ear heard,
> Nor have entered into the heart of man
> The things which God has prepared for those who love Him."

But God has revealed them to us through His Spirit.
For the Spirit searches all things, yes, the deep things of
God... Now we have received, not the spirit of the world,
but the Spirit who is from God, **that we might know the
things that have been freely given to us by God.** (1
Corinthians 2:9-10, 12, NKJV)

The ability to know by the Holy Spirit what are the
"things to come" (John 16:13) are not just for the purpose of
having that knowledge. The Holy Spirit does not give
knowledge of the future for knowledge's sake. He gives it for
love's sake. He knows that knowledge alone will puff up, but
love will build up (1 Cor. 8:1). And what better way to build
our love than to show us what policies, products, songs, books,
businesses, medical discoveries, or educational programs that
will be needed in the future to impact millions of people with
the purpose of making this world look like Heaven?

If your heart and love for everyone who is made in the
image of God does not increase as you seek for disclosure of
the future, then it could be because you are stepping into your
partnership with the Holy Spirit with a selfish intent. We
cannot be surprised if He does not show us anything of the
things to come if our hearts are only focusing on our kingdom
instead of His Kingdom. But if your desire for generational
impact and legacy increases with your pursuit, then it will not

117

be long before He shows you things that will radically transform people's lives.

For me personally, as I began writing out this book, something inside of me stirred up for a deeper understanding of what this could become. It was several weeks of seeking the Holy Spirit for the answer to this inward prompting that He showed me that this was my life message.

The message of rulership is the thing I would define my life by, and He showed me what it could be beyond the book. That was confirmed after Chantal read the first draft of the manuscript and told me, "Babe, I don't think you just found your life message, I think you found *our* life message and our *family's* life message. This will be what our children will embody growing up."

Those words marked my soul as a confirmation that the Holy Spirit wants this message to be more than a book. He wants it to become a movement and that is precisely why we have started Born To Rule Global©. We will be providing Born To Rule coaching (all about high performance and ruling every area of your life), conferences, books, live and virtual events, e-courses, church and business consulting, and merch.

There are so many plans that have been written down about what the future will look like and the millions of people who will be impacted. The anchoring question I have developed for this endeavor is this: What would it look like if we eradicated false humility in the Body of Christ?

So, go forward with spending time with the Holy Spirit. He is not weird despite what you have been told or have seen with your eyes through the bad example of others. He is wise, will lead you into all truth, will show you the things to come, will speak for you when you do not know what to say, is always interceding for you, will teach you when you ask Him questions, will guide you when you are unsure of what to do, and will strengthen you with supernatural power to be a witness to the world of the preeminence of our King and His Kingdom.

Your freedom from the prison you have been in or the cage you have been stuck in with be a catalyst for the freedom of others. Your spark will combine with the spark of other rulers in the family of God and will usher in the new era of influence the Church will have on the world.

You are not too old or too young to move forward, too deep into tradition or too deep into mistakes to change, too uneducated or too inexperienced to be used by God. You are a king or queen, a child of the Most High, a ruler placed on earth to displace the darkness, and royalty whose birthright is dominion.

Now that we have painted the picture of the effects the message of rulership will have on the Church, on the world, and on you, let's move on to the practical ways you can rule your internal world – your mind, heart, and hands – and rewire them for dominion.

Key Principles

1. Since the Church is the people, then the collective body of believers are not changed until the individual believer is changed.

2. When you make the commitment to reclaim your God-given birthright to rule on earth, then every area of your life will be revitalized.

3. God does not send revival. He sends His Holy Spirit to fill us and we become revival.

4. Revival is not an event waiting to happen, it is an identity waiting to be accepted.

5. Your identity as a ruler was intended for you to walk in relational-rulership with the King of kings and the One that is more powerful than you.

6. The difference between a person with power and a person with authority is that the man or woman who possesses authority is someone who has their identity co-signed by God.

7. Don't be intimidated by successful people or those who outwardly have things together. When things are going bad spiritually, you are the spiritual authority God has placed to handle those things.

8. Feeling hopeless, powerless, or trapped are all byproducts of us encountering a situation that causes us to think there is not a solution.

9. As one makes the journey to change from being a victim to being a ruler, a mindset shift takes place from an external locus of control to an internal locus of control.

10. Everything is "figureoutable".

11. The amount of adversity you overcome directly affects the weight of the spiritual authority you possess.

12. The Holy Spirit does not give knowledge of the future for knowledge's sake. He gives it for love's sake.

13. What would it look like if we eradicated false humility in the Body of Christ?

Rewiring Your Mind for Rulership

"Christian, I can't believe you like doing that."

"I don't. I actually hate it."

"So why are you doing it, then?"

"Because it's one of those things that is good for me and I know I will grow to like it."

This was one of the frequent conversations my wife and I have about all of the random things I do or the things I take to enhance my mind and body. This particular exchange was about the cold showers I force myself to take every morning.

My response to Chantal's straightforward remark of her disbelief and my apparent enjoyment of cold water shows an important fact: we don't have to like something to live out a lifestyle that is beneficial for our lives.

123

To drive this point even further, I despised cold water because of the discomfort it presented, but this discomfort was actually born out of my unfamiliarity with cold showers. In fact, my comfort zone with showers had always been the opposite - scathing hot water burning my skin.

But things were beginning to change the more time I spent exercising my willpower to subject my body to the freezing water every morning. It moved from pain to mild discomfort to acute enjoyment to intense love. The more I stood under the water, the more my pain changed into pleasure.

What I noticed, however, was that the change would only occur under one condition: my body would sense the surge of energy, strength and vitality only when the water hit my head or face. In other words, I would just be downright cold if I limited the exposure of the water to just my body. When I allowed my head and face to be in direct contact with the stream, that is when the change in my body occurred.

It is no surprise that before my heart could receive a surplus amount of energy to supply my hands with the strength to carry out objectives for the day, my head must be touched first. In essence, before our hearts and hands can be transformed to live in dominion, our minds must be rewired.

There are plenty of reasons why we need to rewire our minds for dominion before touching the heart and hands. Still, there is one reason of primary importance: the power our beliefs have on us. Everything begins and ends with the mind. What we have in our heads is more than just a brain; it is an entire ecosystem or community of beliefs. And our beliefs shape every aspect of our lives. We have specific beliefs about self-protection, the value of relationships, how we view ourselves, and our beliefs about God.

Believe it or not, every emotion you feel, and every action you take first began as a belief. And because our feelings, actions, and perspectives are built on the foundations of our beliefs, that means we cannot elevate above them. The formula for the power of the beliefs in your mind goes like this:

Beliefs ➡ Thoughts & Perspectives ➡ Emotions ➡ Actions & Words ➡ Life

In simplest terms, you make your beliefs, and then your beliefs make you. If you believe you are dumb, then you will always pass the responsibility of decisions that require thinking to other people. If you believe that life must be very difficult for it to be from God, then you will create greater obstacles or self-sabotage just to experience a bit of pain and resistance to validate your "sufferings for Christ."

The opposite is also true. When you possess a mindset that expects good to be worked in your favor, then you can have pure joy when obstacles occur because you know greater breakthroughs and opportunities are born out of crises. When you expect to make an impact in every room you step into because you are a part of the Royal Family of Heaven, you will not sense the intimidation that is often present with those who see themselves in a self-deprecating light when you are amongst the rich and influential.

Even Paul knew how much power is present with the act of rewiring and renewing the mind.

> And do not be conformed to this world, but be transformed by the **renewing** of your mind, that you may prove what is that good and acceptable and perfect will of God. (Romans 12:2, NKJV)

When our beliefs are transformed, then our heart receives the energy it needs to empower our hands to take dominion over every area of our lives. Our entire world - family, friends, career, church, city, country - is forever changed all because you chose to change what you believe in your head. If you do not believe me on this, ask yourself this question: what separates us from every other animal or creature that lives on this earth and that is directly linked to our ability to dominate this planet?

It is not our strength that separates us. Lions, elephants, and countless other animals beat us in that category. It is not our ability to breathe under water. Our inability to live a long time does not separate us, as plenty of other animals can survive a nuclear attack or live longer than 120 years. If it is not our strength, our inability to breathe under water, or our relativity fragile life, then what truly creates that distinction and gives us the advantage over every living thing on the earth? It is our minds.

Even though we do not know how to fly, we have used our minds to create planes to soar higher, longer, and farther in the air than any eagle could ever imagine. Even if a majority of human beings cannot hold their breath for more than one minute, we have designed submarines to be underneath the water for long periods of time and produced large cruise ships for people to vacation on for weeks at a time in the middle of the ocean. The massive gap between us and every other animal is the power of our minds.

In order to rewire our powerful minds, we must take one thing to heart: you should not fight against your beliefs, you should just upgrade them. One of the worst things any child of God can do is spend countless days, weeks, months, or years fighting against their mind instead of upgrading them by installing new beliefs. Your mind developed the current beliefs you possess through decades of experiences, relationships, pain, and information, so fighting against them takes more time and energy than it does to focus on giving it a higher belief to accept.

And this is precisely why we are going to go through the 8 Rulership Beliefs together. As we look into them, we will then break each one down individually with the realities present within the Scriptures so you can confidently know the truth that sets you *permanently* free.

8 Rulership Beliefs

1. I am never the victim of my circumstances or surroundings. I am the result of my beliefs.

2. My presence, words, and actions matter and carry weight. I expect things to change because God had me walk in the room.

3. The fullness of God is inside of me through the Holy Spirit.

4. I am royalty and don't have to convince God to come through for me because He already wants to do it.

5. I am a king or queen. I rule on earth in the same way God rules in Heaven.

6. I have the authority, love, and glory that Jesus possessed while on earth.

7. I don't have to prove myself because I'm already approved of by my Father the King.

8. Success is my responsibility, mandate, and birthright.

Let's start with the first one that will ultimately set us up for the other seven.

1. *I am never the victim of my circumstances or surroundings. I am the result of my beliefs.*

This belief is of primary importance because it sets the stage for us to receive or reject every other belief we must rewire. This one is important to grasp in our personal lives since it is ingrained in our actual biology.

There's a specific system in our brains called the Reticular Activity System (RAS) that proves this truth. Its primary function is to protect our brains from being overly stimulated by focusing solely on the things that will bring us survival and eliminating things that aren't important to us.

In other words, it helps you focus on the road in front of you when you are driving while blocking out the cars on the other side, the color of the buildings you pass by, and the hairstyle of the driver in the car next to you. It's also responsible for me noticing Toyota Corollas everywhere after I received it as my first car.

Before I received a Corolla as my first car, I did not notice them around me. I would ride in the car to places, go to the mall, or visit family, and none would catch my attention. It was only after I created the sentimental value in my mind about my first official car that I began to notice them everywhere. The Corollas were always there, but I now was able to notice them since I attributed a value of importance to that type of car now. The same occurred once I began to enjoy Tesla's – I saw them everywhere I went.

How does the RAS tie in with our lives being the result of our beliefs? Simple. This system in our brains is responsible for either seeing a situation as a problem that will crush us or an opportunity that will advance us. It affects only our attention where we observe more often the things we value and believe. It proves this axiom true: the only difference between a stumbling block and a stepping stone is the person who is viewing it.

When you genuinely believe in your soul that nothing you face will defeat you because He who is in you is greater than that in the world (1 John 4:4), then you will notice more solutions when obstacles spring up. When you believe in your heart that you are supposed to be influential, you will discover and attract people who have that same belief.

It is not only in your physical biology, but it is also in your spiritual identity. The Scriptures are clear that whatever you believe about yourself, you become (Proverbs 23:7) and it will directly correlate with your discernment of God's will (Romans 12:2).

The truths you tell yourself will ultimately affect your heart and your hands. Believing life is meant to be hard or you'll never get ahead will produce the exact kind of life you proclaim. Your mind will look for ways to self-sabotage or be connected with people who fit the reality of those beliefs while building up a discomfort if you were to break free from it.

And as you realize your beliefs matter and affect you significantly, it will be easier to embrace this next belief.

2. *My presence, words, and actions matter and carry weight. I expect things to change because God had me walk in the room.*

When you believe your actions, words, and presence matter, you will begin to conduct yourself at a higher standard. Since you understand your words carry weight, you won't lash out in anger at someone knowing you will tear them down.

You will choose to speak life over your situation and other people because your words literally have the power to create life or cause death (Proverbs 18:24). You know that by your actions, generational cycles will be broken (Psalm 145:4; 2 Timothy 1:3-5). Side note: generational cycles are different from generational curses; one takes time to defeat, the other is destroyed immediately at the Cross.

Even Solomon, the wisest king to ever live before Jesus, noted this about the effect people have on the earth when they don't believe everything they do matters,

> For three things the earth is perturbed, yes, for four it cannot bear up: For **a servant when he reigns**, a fool when he is filled with food, a hateful woman when she is married, and **a maidservant who succeeds her mistress**. (Proverbs 30:21-23, NKJV)

Two of those four things that rattle the earth has to do with servants being elevated to rulership status. Why is this bad? Shouldn't we want servants to lead? The lesson behind this verse is not about the heart of a servant but about the mindset of someone who has lived in subjection a majority of their life. When someone has the mindset of a pauper and servant, they do not think they matter, or they feel the need to overcompensate to prove their worth.

If they step into a place of great leadership over others, the environment produced under their reign will be one of tyranny, betrayal or mistrust. Words will be spoken quickly when they should have been weighed carefully. Deprecatory jokes, a harsh environment, or a place of mediocrity will be produced.

The opposite is also correct, however. When someone who possesses the mindset of royalty steps into a position of great leadership over others, you can expect them to live at a higher standard. Because royalty goes through an all-encompassing adolescent education to craft their mindset and weigh their actions and words heavily, they are prepared for greater responsibility.

They inherently know they are made for influence and choose to conduct themselves at a high level. They will use their rulership authority to build people, not take advantage of them or use them for personal gain. It must be the same with you and every other child of the King of the universe.

When you expect your presence, words, and actions to matter and change things, then you will realize that the source of that power and authority rests with the fullness of God living inside of you.

3.   The fullness of God is inside of me through the Holy Spirit.

Yes, you read that right – the fullness of God lives inside of you. You may struggle to believe this due to past mistakes or

135

a lack of influence in your world, but those results do not tell the truth. Just as I may not use a tool in my toolbox to fix something and try to use my bare hands instead, it is the same when we try to face life's situations without the reality of God's fullness inside of us.

If you have said "yes" to Jesus and have the Holy Spirit living inside of you, then you have the fullness of wisdom, power, love, joy, strength, patience the Godhead possesses. For example, if you have Jesus living in your heart (Ephesians 3:17), then you have wisdom beyond all measure inside of you. He even testified about His wisdom when He mentioned He was wiser than Solomon (Matthew 12:42). Even the Holy Spirit is known as the Spirit of wisdom (Isaiah 11:2).

This means any answer you are seeking for is inside of you. It can be found in other voices or books you read, but God's greatest desire is for your eyes to be open to the reality that the answer is within you! If Jesus is in you, then an endless reservoir of wisdom is there, too. You don't need more wisdom, as if you lack it. What you need is more awareness, access, and activation of the wisdom that is already there!

Not only is there wisdom present, but there is an unlimited amount of love and power locked away in your inner man. You have someone on the inside of you that is waiting to be unleashed. Jesus literally restored us to a place of almost being spiritual superheroes. Maybe this is why children innately believe they can be like the superhero they see on the movie screen.

Read these next verses below in Ephesians 3 slowly and let every verse sink into your mind and heart. Replace the lies that you are nobody or powerless with the truth that you are loved and powerful beyond measure in the Kingdom.

> For this reason I bow my knees to the Father of our Lord Jesus Christ, from whom the whole family in heaven and earth is named, that He would grant you, according to the riches of His glory, to be strengthened **with might through His Spirit in the inner man**, that Christ may dwell in your hearts through faith; that you, being rooted and grounded in love, may be able to comprehend with all the saints what *is* the width and length and depth and height— to know the love of Christ which passes knowledge; **that you may be filled with all the fullness of God.** Now to Him who is able to do exceedingly abundantly above all that we ask or think, according to the power that works in us, Ephesians 3:14-20 (NKJV)

As you choose today to look at yourself in the mirror as the vessel which God chose to fill up with all that He is, let's allow the identity given by Him permeate our entire being.

4. *I am royalty and don't have to convince God to come through for me because He already wants to do it.*

When a king has a family, his children are called princes and princesses. They are born into an influential family treated with love and respect and brought up in an educational system to prepare them for rulership. As the time for dinner would be commence, every prince and princess would sit at the table with their father, eat the exact same delicacies as the King and ask for more without being condemned or shunned.

When the King of the universe had children, they became the Royal Family of Heaven. Those who took on the family name instantly received adoption, and all of the family benefits. These family benefits also include being a co-heir of the Kingdom alongside Jesus (Romans 8:17). Since you took on the name of the Son, Christ, then you became royalty as He is.

You are not God's slaves or servants; you are His son or daughter. You are royalty now. Your identity is not assigned to a peasant in the field, but a child in the palace. You do not need to cower behind small petitions because you feel it's prideful or evil to pray big, specific prayers. You can access his throne with confidence and boldness (Ephesians 3:11-12), ask Him for great things, and not feel bad about it. There is no need to hide behind timidity, and a lack of faith that we often proclaim to be a display of humility when it is really false humility.

You are so valuable to the King that Jesus sends angels to serve and assist you (Hebrews 1:14), was not ashamed to call you brother or sister (Hebrews 2:11) and did not mind raising you up to glory (Hebrews 2:10). As your mind shifts from being a slave to royalty, then accepting your position as a ruler is the next step.

5. *I am a king or queen. I rule on earth in the same way God rules in Heaven.*

As we have traversed throughout the narrative of Genesis, we have discovered God's primary intention for Man was that of rulership. He sought for Man to live with dominion over the world He created and to rule as He ruled Heaven.

After the fall of Man, Jesus came to shed His blood as a perfect sacrifice to make us holy again so the Holy Spirit could invade the inside of us. As the Spirit of God completed His invasion, Man was given back the rightful authority to rule as kings and queens under the King of Kings. Even the apostle John echoes sentiment by definitively declaring,

> To Him who loved us and washed us from our sins in His own blood and has made us **kings** and **priests** to His God and Father, to Him be glory and dominion forever and ever. Amen. (Revelation 1:5b-6, NKJV)

Yes, you read that correctly. The blood of Jesus on the Cross has made us kings and priests unto God. This means rulership runs in your blood. It means you possess royal authority on earth to function as you see your Father operate. You mirror Him in every way like Jesus did (John 5:19).

When problems arise, your Father does not lose His composure and, thus, you should not either. When opposition rises up, your Father does not shrink back, and therefore, you should not either. When situations call for a wise decision, your Father does not rush to make one and, consequently, you should not either.

The more you keep your eyes fixed on how your Father responds and rules, then the more you will experience the results He intended for you. It is impossible to not rule with the wisdom, strength, passion, clarity, creativity, joy and love of God without experiencing the favor, power, anointing, and results of God. And, believe it or not, your Father wants you to be successful so rule like He does. Take up your mandate as a king or queen under the King of Kings. Your life will change dramatically because of this one decision. I know this decision changed mine.

And if you believe being given the position of king and priest under God is a breathtaking thing, wait until you see the Scriptures that confirm the next belief.

6. *I have the authority, love, and glory that Jesus possessed while on earth.*

You might not know this, but Jesus left you more than just a golden ticket to get to Heaven. He left us with a mandate to disciple the entire earth to obey the King. And with that mandate – which is known as the Great Commission - He left us His authority, love and glory to aid us in the fulfillment of this mission.

As it pertains to His authority, a resurrected Christ is about to ascend into Heaven and right before He leaves, He proclaims to His disciples that all authority has been given to Him. We are to go in His name - names in ancient times included covering, blessing, and authority - to change nations (Matthew 28:18-20). If that's not overwhelming enough, look at what is said about us when Jesus heals a lame man in Matthew 9.

> 'But that you may know that the **Son of Man** has **authority** on earth to forgive sins'—he then said to the paralytic—'Rise, pick up your bed and go home.' And he rose and went home. When the crowds saw it, they were afraid, and they glorified God, who had given such **authority** to men. (Matthew 9:6-8, ESV)

Stumbling upon that verse for the first time a few years ago, I needed to read it a few times to make sure I didn't miss anything. I hope you are in the same disbelief now as I was back then. Shocks to our paradigms are always healthy when we are brought back to the elevated place Jesus designed us to live in instead of the lower level we have chosen to settle on.

And if possessing the same authority Jesus had here on earth wasn't enough to cause you to view yourself differently, then how would it feel discovering that you are loved by the Father with the same love He loved Jesus? Well, it's true. Jesus Himself prayed for that!

> 'And I have declared to them Your name, and will declare *it,* that **the love with which You loved Me may be in them,** and I in them.' (John 17:26, NKJV)

There it is in plain sight. You are loved the same way Jesus was loved. This simply means you are loved far beyond words can explain nor actions can display. But Jesus doesn't stop there. A few moments earlier, He makes the mind-blowing decision to give us His glory!

In the beginning of His final intercessory prayer, Jesus asks the Father to glorify Him with the identical glory He possessed before the foundation of the world (John 17:5). As He continues with His prayer, He receives the assurance that this request has been approved of and proceeds to give it to us!

> 'And **the glory which You gave Me I have given them**, that they may be one just as We are one' (John 17:22, NKJV)

As we make the decision to stand with the other rulers in the family of God and seek to manifest Heaven on earth in unity, the same glory Jesus had in the beginning of the world will manifest through us. Our King is so wise to put a prerequisite of complete unity as the doorway to accessing His glory set aside for us. There are two prevalent reasons for this.

The first reason why we will not receive His glory without unity is because if only one person could carry His glory, then that person could be set up for the same downfall of pride Lucifer fell under. Thoughts of independence and self-reliance would poison their soul. The second reason why is because His glory is so weighty that if only one person tried to carry it by themselves, it would crush them. God never desired for His glory to be carried by one singular person because He designed His blessings to build us, not destroy us.

And the priority of being completely united in heart and soul under one mission is exactly what the disciples achieved in the Book of Acts. As a result of their unity, shadows and handkerchiefs healed sick people, cities were flipped upside down, dead people were raised to life, and kings were converted. The manifest glory of Jesus could be felt by the entire civilized world through them. Wouldn't you like to be a part of a move of God like that today?

So, there you have it. You have literally been given the authority, love, and glory of Jesus. You are a carrier of those precious, heavenly gifts. Accept them into your mind so it can transform your heart and empower your hands.

Once you fully embrace this truth, you will live your days on this earth with the approval of your Father.

7. I don't have to prove myself because I'm already approved of by my Father the King.

If you have received the same love from the Father that Jesus received, then it also means we have received the same approval He received while on earth. This is shown right after Jesus was baptized by His cousin, John.

> When He had been baptized, Jesus came up immediately from the water; and behold, the heavens were opened to Him, and He saw the Spirit of God descending like a dove and alighting upon Him. And suddenly a voice came from

145

> heaven, saying, '**This is My beloved Son, in whom I am well pleased.**' (Matthew 3:16-17, NKJV)

The empowering truth about the approval of Jesus received at this moment from His Father was that this approval came before He performed any miracles. He did not heal the sick, feed the multitude, nor raise the dead yet.

Do you know what this tells us? That the approval and affirmation the Father has for us has more to do with our position in the family than the performance of our faith. We don't live supernatural lives or do miracles to *receive* His approval but live this way *because* of His approval. Simply put, you are fully approved of and affirmed because of your identity as His child, not due to your ability to live perfectly.

How would your self-talk and thoughts change if you loved and approved of yourself the same amount God does? How much would your self-worth raise up if you allow yourself to be built the way the Father wants to build you up? I have a strong feeling that your mind would drastically change into a more affirming inner world. One that feeds you instead of drains and attacks you.

Well, it's about time to make the surrender. It's time to stop speaking words over yourself God Himself wouldn't even say. It's time to no longer try to oppose the constant changing opinions of others and stop seeking to prove yourself because you are already approved of.

Today is the day to make the choice to finally be secure in who you are. You need to love your crazy quirks and your dry humor - I have very dry humor, you can ask my wife. The only thing that needs to grow and change is our character. And this is done by going after wisdom, not by attacking ourselves. Embrace the output of your personality. Surrender the image of your character. Love and approve of yourself because the Father already does.

Now it is time to move on to this last belief, which may be the hardest to believe and accept.

8.   *Success is my responsibility, mandate, and birthright.*

When God formed Adam and Eve out of His eternal seed, He did not bring them into the world for them to be mediocre. As Jehovah proclaimed, "Let Us make man in Our image and let them have dominion (Genesis 1:26)," in His mind there was an expectation for Man to be successful in all of his endeavors. After all, a father knows deep down that his children will display the qualities he possesses.

Adam and Eve's birthright - privileges and rights given at birth - was to be successful and rule. Because they were infused with the spiritual DNA of the Creator, their lives would only be appropriately expressed if rulership manifested. If the opposite manifested, then they would malfunction – which literally means to not function according to the original design - through anger, depression, anxiety, worry, suicidal thoughts.

This is also why success is our mandate and responsibility. If we are a reflection of Heaven and God's representatives on earth, then would it make sense if God Almighty's children were not influential, successful, and mediocre?

The first time this came across my soul, I rejected it immediately. I proclaimed this to be pride, greed, and evil. But

I soon realized that I sought to dismiss it, not on the basis of pride but because of my false humility. I did not think that being successful held any virtue. In fact, I was taught to believe that the poorer and the more I "barely made it", then the more spiritual and closer to God I was.

That is the opposite of the truth. God explicitly states in Deuteronomy 28:14 that if we follow all of His commandments, His blessings will overtake us. They wouldn't just sprinkle on us, but overwhelm us like a flood. And if that is the Old Covenant, how much greater are His blessings in the New Covenant? It even says in Romans 8:32,

> He who did not spare His own Son, but delivered Him up for us all, how shall He not with Him also **freely give us all things**? (Romans 8:32, NKJV)

This verse clearly states that God will give us all things since He gave us His most valuable possession - His Son. If God already gave us His best gift and His only Son, why won't He provide us with everything else including success - especially considering that success is not even close to the value of having Jesus?

It is false humility that whispers the lies that you are not called to be successful. The promises we proclaim over ourselves of "being the head, not the tail" (Deut. 28:13) and "no weapon formed against us shall prosper" (Isaiah 54:17) are said with no resistance because they are spoken with the mentality of just surviving. What if we began to proclaim these promises over our lives because of the desire to thrive, not just survive? Make no mistake: if you have Christ in your life, are filled with the Holy Spirit, and are infused with the spiritual DNA of your Creator, then success is your responsibility, mandate, and birthright.

This chapter is heavy because of the complete rewiring that must take place in our minds with our beliefs. Take fifteen minutes every morning and speak them over yourself. Close your eyes and visualize each belief coming into fruition throughout your day. Note what you see, hear, taste, and smell during this time. Let your thoughts be enveloped with these beliefs and watch how different your thought processes will be.

You will be sharper, more confident, less anxious, filled with greater peace, and more sensitive to the Holy Spirit. And finally, you'll get to experience the freedom present when your mind works with and for you instead of against you. Now that we have taken the time to rewire your mind for dominion, let's do the same thing for your heart.

Key Principles

1. Our minds must first be rewired before our hearts and hands can be transformed to live in dominion.

2. Every emotion we feel and every action we take first began as a belief.

3. You make your beliefs and then your beliefs make you.

4. Do not fight against your beliefs, simply upgrade them.

5. Use the 8 Rulership Beliefs to upgrade your mind.

6. Use your rulership authority to build people, not take advantage of them or use them for personal gain.

7. Your identity is not assigned to a peasant in the field, but a child in the palace.

8. The more you keep your eyes fixed on how your Father responds and rules, then the more you will experience the results He intended for you.

9. God designed His blessings to build us, not destroy us.

10. You are affirmed and approved of because of your position in the family, not the performance of your faith.

11. It is false humility that whispers the lie that you are not called to be successful.

12. Take 15 minutes every morning and speak the Rulership Beliefs over yourself. Best practices would include closing your eyes and visualizing the belief coming into fruition.

Reshaping Your Heart for Rulership

As a person who is invigorated by the use of my mind in accelerating the capabilities of my brain, writing and principles centered around the heart do not come easy. In fact, it is much easier for me to be impassioned about a topic or situation with my heart for a few moments only to retreat back into the safe haven of my mind.

Vulnerability, gratitude, and heartfelt love that brings one to tears has been something I've needed to develop to live the full life King Jesus planned for me. This shift from rejecting my heart to embracing it came as a result of the discovery of the plans laid out for me.

> The thief does not come except to steal, and to kill, and to destroy. I have come that they may have **life**, and that they may have it **more abundantly**. (John 10:10, NKJV)

God and Satan both have plans for our lives. One of them is oriented towards stealing, killing, and destroying while the other is geared towards abundant living. What caused me to pay more attention to my emotions was the fact that the object of these plans coming into fruition all centered around the heart.

In simplest terms, the place of focus where both Jesus and Satan direct their influence is the spiritual aspect of the organ beating in your chest. Just as the brain contains the spiritual component of the mind, so our physical beating heart carries a spiritual element in the word "heart" that is used in the Bible - which is the seat of emotions from where we rule and make decisions. It is the central aspect of a person's ability to experience God or Satan's plan for their life. It is so vital that even King Solomon - the wisest man before Jesus - proclaimed,

> Keep your **heart** with all diligence, for out of
> it spring the issues of life. (Proverbs 4:23, NKJV)

The massive importance of the heart does not discount the importance of the mind. It can be so easy to dismiss the previous chapter after hearing that the ability to experience God's goodness lies in our hearts, but do not make that mistake. One of the ways to guard the heart is to continually renew the beliefs of the mind. Renewing your mind actually protects the state or condition of your heart. Without this, your heart can be bitter when it should be free, sad when it should be joyful, hopeless when it should be encouraged.

We cannot live out the rulership mandate on our lives if we do not subdue every area - mind, heart, and hands. So do not throw out the rulership beliefs. They ultimately create the foundation the heart builds upon.

And as we embrace the power we possess when our hearts are healed, full, and healthy by implementing the principles we will share together, you will see your life come alive again. Colors will burst, joy will fill your heart, friendships will finally fulfill you, and you will encounter the lasting and deep unconditional love the Father has for you.

This is why God said that we would find Him if we sought Him with all of our hearts. It is because when we combine the dynamic effects our emotions have with the truth of His Word amid our intimate bond with Him, it changes everything.

> And you will seek Me and find Me, when you search for Me with all your **heart**. (Jeremiah 29:13, NKJV)

Our hearts have such a great effect on our lives that God literally says you will find Him when you seek Him with it. Think about it: The Creator of the universe says you can encounter Him when you focus on your heart. This truth reminds me of the time when my wife and I bought some food and drove to a parking lot that overlooked the sunset in Dana Point, CA. As the red-orange streaks appeared across the sky and the sun began to set, I heard this whisper from the Holy Spirit: "You will find more of *My* heart when you are willing to return back to *your* heart."

That floored me. I instantly felt a flood of emotions and tears welled up in my eyes. Chantal turned towards me and saw them appear and hugged me deeply without feeling the need to say anything. The next day, I attempted to process what occurred the night before because of one simple fact: I was taught that my heart was evil and always deceitful. I grew up learning not to trust my heart, no matter how mature I had been in my walk with Christ. But what the Holy Spirit whispered to me caused me to deep dive into the Scriptures to uncover the truth, and honestly, I'm glad I did.

Now before we jump into the truth together about your heart, you may need to do the same thing I did. I had to make the conscious decision that in order to discover the truth which sets me free, I needed to be willing to accept that my presuppositions, or previous beliefs, could be wrong. It is easier said than done because many of us, me included, had good-intentioned people who genuinely loved God teach us this. Their awe-inspiring love for our King made it simple for me to receive it without any reservation nor reading the Scriptures for myself on this matter.

But as time went on and I searched for the truth, I was able to discover God's perspective on my born-again heart. Even though I made this discovery, it still took time for the wisdom to travel from my head to my heart. I accepted the truth about my heart within a matter of days, but I did not really begin to trust my heart until months later. This is how ingrained beliefs work. It may take months for the heart to catch up even after the mind has already changed course. This is why we still sense the emotions of unforgiveness long after we have made the conscious decision to forgive the person who deeply wounded us.

So, without further ado, let's make our way towards reshaping our hearts by rediscovering the goodness of it.

New Nature, New Heart

When Adam and Eve sinned against the King, they opened the doorway for their nature to be distorted. Once their nature changed from holy to sinful, their hearts soon followed. And this destructive transformation affected far more than the first two people to walk in rulership on the earth; it touched everyone who would fall in their lineage - that's you and me.

Since we were fashioned by God to exercise dominion over the earth the way He rules in Heaven, we needed redemption. Since God is a holy, just creator, and a king, He must punish traitors who have sinned against Him. A king must execute justice towards any unrighteousness if their kingdom will last (Proverbs 16:12, 25:5) and if their glory will spread to cover the earth (Proverbs 14:34).

However, because God loved us so dearly (John 3:16, Romans 5:8) and would not retract giving us dominion

(Genesis 1:26), He chose to come as a man Himself to pay the ultimate price we could not pay. Since the first Adam used his will to indulge in sin, the last Adam used His will to overcome it.

Due to the sacrifice and resurrection of Jesus, those who would say "yes" to Him and become children of God are given the opportunity to have their nature and heart changed. This truth is echoed in the prophetic promise God gives us through Ezekiel.

> I will give you a **new heart** and put a **new spirit** within you; I will take the heart of stone out of your flesh and give you a heart of flesh. I will put My Spirit within you and cause you to walk in My statutes, and you will keep My judgments and do them. (Ezekiel 36:26-27, NKJV)

What is noteworthy here is the context of the word "spirit" is the word *ruach* in Hebrew. In both verses, it uses that same word for the phrases "new spirit" and "my Spirit." The same term is used for multiple things, including the Holy Spirit, attitude, mind, and many others. With these verses, the meaning differs. In verse 27, God genuinely speaks about putting His Spirit (uppercase 'S'), the Holy Spirit, inside of us to be able to follow Him. But in the verse preceding it, the word "spirit" (lowercase 's') means the mode of thinking and acting for a person.

As you can see, God prophetically speaks that when His salvation appears, He will give us a new heart and a new mode of thinking and action due to the infilling of His Spirit. In other words, when the Holy Spirit lives inside of you after the complete surrender to King Jesus, then you are born again with a new heart and new nature.

You begin to be burdened for things you did not care about before. You now see circumstances in a new light and understanding you did not have before. You can no longer do the same things or sin the same way with relative ease. You have a new heart and nature now.

This is why the Holy Spirit whispered to me about returning back to my heart. I needed to realize that my heart yearned for the Kingdom and His presence. It wanted to see Heaven manifest on the earth in dramatic ways. It yearned for the glory of God to be displayed through miracles and wonders. It longed to see the next great move of revival the

Father wants to unleash in this world – and it still does to this day with an unquenchable fire.

But, just as with any child, you don't jump all in and proclaim every passion or emotion as truth. There's a link between innocence and immaturity. When babies are born, they need instruction on how to operate properly on earth. They have no previous experience and they need other adults to teach them that it's not a good idea to touch a hot stove or to run in the middle of the street when a ball bounces in that direction.

Their lack of maturity and wisdom proves they need instruction and a community of other people to walk with them. This does not, however, point to them being evil or deceitful. In the same way that babies aren't regarded as evil but immature, so we too must regard born-again believers are immature and not evil. Our new hearts are not evil in nature, but immature and in need of wisdom.

That is why there is a prevalent need in every Christian's life for wise community, consistent and heartfelt prayer life, reading and understanding the Scriptures, and opportunities to serve to outwork what has been placed within us. For me personally, this fresh understanding of my heart allows me to trust the inherent desires it possesses but also helps me recognize the need to bring in other voices to speak as to why I desire for that specific thing or how to go about fulfilling it.

And yet the truth remains, your heart wants God's goodness in your life. It wants to live holy and impact people for eternity. It wants to be so close to Jesus that you can feel His heartbeat. Trust your heart and begin to see it as inherently good because it is. When you do that, you will experience the endless joy, peace, and love Jesus desired for you. You will no longer search for external things to fill you but will be able to possess a heart that's always full.

Now that we've settled the reality that your heart is trustworthy after salvation and is the key to walking in the fullness of dominion, let's complete these steps to reshape our hearts back to its original position.

1. *Forgive Quickly.*

There are countless books and sermons dedicated to the power of forgiveness, so I will not dive deep into the subject. However, what I will address is that the ploy and tactic Satan uses to gain a foothold in our hearts is in the area of offense.

Now for us to fully grasp forgiveness and live it out, we must differentiate between "offense" and "being offended". Here's the difference: offense is an event or action while being offended is a choice.

One of the things my wife used to hate during our first year of marriage was when I never took responsibility for her reactions, only my actions and words. Whenever she said, "You made me angry or hurt or offended," I would sharply respond, "Babe, I didn't make you do anything. You made a choice to respond that way."

She obviously did not appreciate my response in the moment, as it caused the heated discussion to persist longer than it needed to. Still, later on, she admitted I was right. Fast forward to 5 years later at the time of this writing, and we now take responsibility for our words and actions without assigning blame to the other party. We have a vibrant, powerful marriage as a result.

It is untrue that someone can "make" us do anything. Either we allow them access to our hearts, and we make the decision to hold onto the offense, or we release it to God knowing that we flourish when we operate according to our design. We were born to rule everything – both external and internal. When God told Adam and Eve to subdue everything (subdue means to "bring under control" or "overcome by force"), it meant that they would never be ruled by anything else other than Him.

Can anger subdue us? Absolutely. Can bitterness control us? Yes, it can. Can unforgiveness hold us back? Absolutely. On the contrary, the only thing that is allowed and permitted to subdue our hearts is love because *God* is love. Only peace and joy are permitted because that is the fruit of the Holy Spirit – which again is God.

Since God is the only One who is the King of Kings and is correctly above us, He is the only Person we allow ourselves to be subdued by. That means every quality He brings is allowed to be inside of us. This does not include anger without a cause nor bitterness and slander of others.

So, make the choice today to forgive quickly and to stop holding things against people. Satan wants you to do the opposite because he desires access to your dominion power. Don't let him gain a foothold in your heart (Ephesians 4:26-27, 2 Corinthians 2:10-11).

2.   *Meditate on His Goodness and Promises.*

Meditation is not something that originates in New Age practices or Buddhism to achieve Nirvana. God prescribed this as an active way of recollection for His people so they would not stray from His commands.

> This Book of the Law shall not depart from your mouth, but you **shall meditate in it day and night**, that you may observe to do according to all that is written in it. For then you will make your way prosperous, and then you will have good success. (Joshua 1:8, NKJV)

The directive to Joshua about meditating on God's promises precedes the famous verse 9 many of us know by heart. What's striking about this verse before it lies in the effects Joshua's meditation would have on his life. Let's reread verse 8 to discover the powerful effect behind meditating on His promises.

> This Book of the Law shall not depart from your mouth, but you shall meditate in it day and night, that you may observe to do according to all that is written in it. For then **you will make your way** prosperous, and then you will have good success. (Joshua 1:8, NKJV)

God literally told Joshua that if he meditated on His promises, then Joshua himself would make his own way prosperous and successful. God never said to Joshua that He would make the conqueror's way prosperous and successful, but Joshua would for himself!

In other words, God's words would soak so deeply into the innermost parts of his heart that as he went on forward, he could take dominion and conquer as a natural byproduct. It is likened to why God brought animals for Adam to name and then stepped back. Adam had so much of his Father's image and likeness that the Lord observed from afar and did not interfere. This is the power of meditating on His promises: you will be so empowered by His goodness that you couldn't help *but* be successful. You would not need to use the phrase, "If it's Your will, God" because you would clearly see that it is!

Now, this begs the question: how do I properly meditate? Try these three simple steps you can do in fifteen minutes.

First, be still and put your mind on God. Do you know what you're *not* thinking about? The bills you have to pay or the fight you just had with a loved one. Do not move onto the second step until you begin to experience peace from putting your mind on God. If you're still anxious, worried, sad or angry, stay there for a few moments longer.

Second, choose one promise to meditate on for a few minutes. It could be your promise to be an influential politician, your family being financially free, completing that doctoral program you have not registered for yet, or finishing that book you're supposed to write.

And finally, begin to visualize the promise *already* in fruition. In other words, begin to thank God for its fulfillment as if you are already in possession of it. Then you can end the session once you sense a release in your heart by the Holy Spirit.

These steps may seem difficult or counterproductive at first, but don't rush it. Your heart is powerfully impacted by the words you tell yourself and the images you show yourself. As a result, if you continuously show your heart God's promises and goodness coming into fruition, it will be ready to subdue anything on the outside world that contradicts this reality.

3. Develop the Practice of Gratitude.

Gratitude is one of the most powerful emotions that is dormant within our hearts. Some say that it is the strongest emotion that can lift the heart above its current state. Whether or not this is true, one thing is for certain - you cannot hope to live fully awake and as a ruler of your world without being in constant supply of gratitude in your daily life.

Here's how I know: God explicitly links gratitude to the flourishing of life. In Philippians 4, Paul connects prayer and gratitude to the ability to receive peace.

> Be anxious for nothing, but in everything by **prayer** and **supplication**, with **thanksgiving**, let your requests be made known to God; and the **peace** of God, which

surpasses all understanding, will guard your hearts and minds through Christ Jesus. (Philippians 4:6-7, NKJV)

The picture here is not to offer up requests you have to God in a way that's laden with unbelief. In order to receive the peace that surpasses all understanding, you need to possess so much faith about the obstacle that you begin to thank God as if He already gave it to you.

Gratitude is needed, therefore, because it is the highest emotional expression of faith towards God. When you close your eyes to the physical realm to approach God in the unseen realm and thank Him for everything He's given you ahead of time, it will only be a matter of time before you receive it in your daily life.

Here's why: in the spiritual realm, there is no past, present or future. There's only the eternal now - which is why God calls Himself the I AM, not the I WAS or the I WILL BE. Since all of God's promises are already in your possession in the unseen realm, what allows Heaven to manifest on earth is your gratitude. This is echoed in Psalm 50,

> 'Offer to God **thanksgiving** and pay your vows to the Most High. Call upon Me in the day of trouble; I **will**

> **deliver you**, and you shall glorify Me.' (Psalm 50:14-15, NKJV)

I vividly remember this happening to me. Chantal and I wanted to bless a few friends with money who needed it for various reasons. The only problem was that it was during the pandemic and we needed an extra $1,000 along with the money necessary to satisfy our needs. I planned diligently and cut out many unnecessary things out of our budget – I must admit, I was operating under a cheap mindset, not an abundant one.

All in all, we made a plan to be able to give the extra money in five months. We thought this was a wise, disciplined plan. We high-fived each other and felt immense gratitude to be able to be generous, even if that generosity is planned over time. Still, as with many plans Chantal and I have created in the past, God had other ideas.

The next morning, as I began to pray, I heard God whisper to me:

> "Christian, for the money you want to give, how long will it take for you to save it?"

"Well Lord, it'll take us five months to save the extra $1000 we want to give."

"So why don't you ask Me for it? It's much faster than waiting."

It was in that moment where I was struck by the simplicity of God. *Is it really that easy?* I thought to myself. After a few moments of wrestling with the ease of the request, I asked Him for the money all the way to the exact amount. It felt uncomfortable at first, but then a peace fell over me.

"Good, Christian. I'm glad you asked Me for it. Now be thankful and grateful as if you already had it in your account to give."

This request to be grateful ahead of time seemed foreign to me, so it took me a few hours to even allow it to resonate with my heart. After hours of wrestling with it, I decided to obey with my whole heart and not with my skepticism. As I began to thank Him the next day for the money, I sensed a massive shift occurring in my heart where I experienced a flood of emotions that caused me to weep with joy and smile bigger than I had in months.

Not only did my heart burst with love and power, but we ended up receiving an extra check in the mail two weeks later that covered what we wanted to give and more – and no, it was not a government stimulus check. Being grateful surely beat having us cut every area of our budget just to stay on track to offer it in five months.

Develop the practice of gratitude in your life. You know you're doing it right when you actually feel the emotions in your heart as opposed to only being stimulated in your mind. God used gratitude to change my life and wants to do the same with yours.

4.   *Limit your exposure to negative people, information, and events.*

Growing up in a Pentecostal youth group filled with passionate teenagers, the constant phrase that was thrown around was, "guard your heart." When this phrase was shared on the pulpit or in conversation, it was usually limited to the area of relationship and purity. Even if you were not interested in someone of the opposite gender, you would be told to "guard your heart" if you were found having an in-depth one-on-one conversation with them.

This kind of regulation and teaching caused me to limit the usefulness of "guarding my heart" solely to sexual purity and relationships with other women. But that cannot be further from the truth. To solely limit this phrase to that one dominant area is to set your heart up for failure to function properly as you get older. This is because the bombardment of events, information, and deepening relationships later on in life will affect your heart in more ways than you will want them to. To truly "guard your heart," you must be willing to limit its exposure to things that don't feed you.

For example, we do not need to watch seven videos, read three articles and argue on seven social media threads to be aware of an event or information. This isn't being prudent; it's being nosy or unwise. When we justify it to ourselves why we need to be consumed with an endless amount of people, information, or events, then we cannot be surprised when our hearts are just as toxic as the things we observe or take in. Remember that whatever excuse we fight for we get to keep.

Hear my heart: I'm not saying that you should live your life ignorant of the rest of the word, but what I am saying is to make the decision to create boundaries around your heart so you can guard it bravely. Guarding your heart is not just limited to sexuality. It also pertains to toxic people, bitterness, overwhelming videos or articles and much more. If it doesn't add to your life and if you notice that your heart isn't producing vibrant, powerful emotions, then it might mean you need less of that one particular thing or relationship than you initially thought.

Answer this question to really see the value of guarding your heart: how would your emotional, mental, and spiritual faculties be if you performed a 14-day negativity fast? If the thought of performing this seems impossible or absurd, the real questions you must answer is: What do you have to lose? And what do you have to gain?

When you make the decision to see your heart as good, realize its importance in exercising your birthright to rule, forgive quickly, spend time deeply meditating on God's promises and goodness, begin to implement the practice of gratitude, and limit the exposure of negativity from information, people, or events, then you will experience the full power God designed for your heart to offer.

You will begin to view your emotions as an asset to exercising your mandate for dominion instead of a hindrance. You will move forward more quickly because you won't spend time discerning whether those passions or ideas are evil. You can regain that awe and wonder of a child that is necessary to walk in the fullness of the abundant Kingdom life. Take the necessary time to reshape your heart, and you will, in turn, take the necessary steps to reshape your life and your world.

Key Principles

1. The object of focus for both God and Satan's plans for our lives are our hearts.

2. Your heart is the seat of emotions from where we rule and make decisions.

3. One of the ways to guard your heart is to continually renew your mind.

4. When you start following Jesus wholeheartedly, you are filled with a new mode of thinking, a new nature, and a new heart.

5. Your heart is not still evil or deceitful after salvation, it is just immature in need of wisdom.

6. One of the biggest ways Satan tries to get access to your heart is through the area of offense.

7. When you meditate on God's laws and goodness, you can't help but be successful.

8. Gratitude is the highest emotional expression of faith towards God.

9. All of God's promises are already in your possession in the unseen realm and what brings them into the physical realm is gratitude.

10. Create boundaries around your heart from toxic sources if you are going to live a vibrant, powerful life.

Retraining Your Hands for Rulership

If you've gotten this far in the book, you would have already discovered your birthright to rule, changed your hardwired beliefs to align with the king or queen you really are, and have reshaped your heart for it to explosively manifest God's plan into your world. This chapter is one of my favorites because it is the one that offers the most practical steps to take. We will be diving into the actions you can take today to experience the results of rulership in your life tomorrow.

The reason we waited till the end is simply that the tools placed in your hands are only as effective as the beliefs in your head and the emotions in your heart. If your beliefs or emotions are not appropriately realigned, then the tool in your hands might be useless or used inappropriately - like one not knowing how to use a hammer (useless) or using it to destroy something instead of build something (inappropriately). Your head and heart matters.

Now that we've rewired your mind and reshaped your heart, it is time to retrain your hands. This is personally exciting because I have experienced the dramatic effects retraining your actions for dominion can have on one's world.

It has allowed me to be in top physical health, helped me develop fulfilling relationships, caused me to step into the places of my purpose, richly supplied me with the discipline necessary to accomplish a lot, and connected me intimately to my King. If this could be done for the guy who would rather do what I want instead of what I need to do, then it can surely be done for you.

Before we jump into the practical actions you can take to retrain your hands, you need to grasp the heart behind them. What we will discuss ahead is all based on the truth of your design. And as we explained in detail before, you were born to rule. When God said for Man to have dominion (Genesis 1:26-28), He called them to subdue everything.

This meant that everything external and internal was designed to submit under our rulership. This means anger issues, neurological difficulties, money, and the like are not intended to subdue us, but to be subdued by us. This is why Jesus does not want us to serve mammon - it is because mammon is supposed to submit to us and serve us, not vice versa. God even echoes that Cain can rule over sin before he infamously kills his brother, Abel,

> So the LORD said to Cain, 'Why are you angry? And why has your countenance fallen? If you do well, will you not be accepted? And if you do not do well, sin lies at the door. And its desire is for you, but **you should rule over it**.' (Genesis 4:6-7, NKJV)

God's suggestion to Cain was to rule over the internal urge to express his anger fueled by rejection. If the Divine Creator suggested an unredeemed Cain should rule over sin, how much more can a fully surrendered and Holy Spirit-filled believer conquer it? Paul shares this straightforward statement when he writes to the Saints in Rome,

> For sin **shall not have dominion** over you, for you are not under law but under grace. (Romans 6:14, NKJV)

God created us to rule over everything that tries to control us. This means choosing to live in such a way that you exercise rulership to achieve optimal success in your physical, mental, emotional, relational, spiritual, financial, and professional life.

It means that your birthright is to have a beautiful relational life with your family, a vibrant spiritual life with King Jesus, a healthy body, heart, and mind, a bountiful bank account and a career that fulfills you to the point that you are fulfilling your eternal destiny. Even the word *Shalom* in the Hebrew language means the full peace of God in every area of your life, not just spiritually.

God explicitly planned for you to be blessed if you chose to obey His commands wholeheartedly and walk in the identity of the ruler you genuinely are. His heart and original intention for you and me were for us to rule our world with such detail, tenacity, strength, love and wisdom that it would reflect how He rules. You were always meant to be like your Father, and now it is time we allow our actions and lives to reflect that fact.

The way we can do this is by taking these three steps:

- Create a plan with God about your life
- Study those who are already living in dominion
- Execute that plan by managing your time and energy

When all of these steps are combined and fully lived out, what you are left with is a life where every area is subdued and under control. You will assume the phrase the Apostle Paul describes us when he says, "we are more than conquerors through Him who loved us" (Romans 8:37).

The life of conquerors means there is consistent war, no peace, and things are always needing to be put back into its proper place. To be more than a conqueror means to live in such a way that there is so much peace, harmony, and synergy in every area of your life that you don't need to war to get your life back in control. In essence, to be more than a conqueror is to be a **ruler**.

This is the essence of what *Shalom* means in the Hebrew. When Jesus wanted to give us peace that the world cannot give (John 14:27), He was speaking to the kind of peace that touches us both now in this life and in the life to come. Now that we have defined what a life of dominion looks like and what being more than a conqueror really means, let's begin retraining our actions to experience the true *Shalom* of God.

1. Create a Plan with God About Your Life.

If we are going to live skillfully - which is the essence of wisdom - as rulers under God, we need an individualized plan or blueprint for our lives. After all, you are called to take dominion over your world in ways that are different than me. This is because each of us has been entrusted with a unique design from God, and we each have varying specifications required for us to maximize our time on earth.

We all are similar in many ways but are also vastly different in other ones. We each need a personalized plan with God to carry out our rulership mandate. This means that in order for your rulership to go forward, you will need to partner with God to create it. Like you, when I first heard the need to plan my life out with God, I cringed at the thought. It seemed counterproductive for me to plan out my life when God had a destiny already designed for me.

That is when I came across this sermon by the late Dr. Myles Munroe about the power of planning. He discussed Proverbs 16:1 and provided two startling truths that opened my eyes as to why planning is vital. We'll touch on them briefly and then talk about practical steps you can take immediately to experience progress.

> The preparations of the heart **belong** to man, but the answer of the tongue is from the LORD. (Proverbs 16:1, NKJV)

Truth #1: Planning is one of the highest physical expressions of faith.

When you are making the decision to plan for anything (a vacation, trip to Disney, road trip, etc.), you are proclaiming that event is a certainty to occur. The purpose of planning is to harness the event or action to get the best out of it. Therefore, when you plan for anything, you are actually performing a declaration of faith over it.

The principle of faith in relation to planning also applies to your life. Since plans belong to us, God describes that we create with Him - not independent of Him - what our lives will look like in great detail. This is the beauty of collaborating with God and operating with a life of faith.

When you plan with God, you please Him because you are operating at a tangible level of faith that is expecting these things to actualize in your life. And as you know, it is impossible to please Him without faith (Hebrews 11:6). But the reverse is also true: audacious levels of faith moves Jesus (Matthew 8:5-13, 15:24-28). This leads to the second truth.

Truth #2: God has a plan for you, but He doesn't plan for you.

Due to us being given the responsibility for our plans, God allows us to live on whatever level of faith we choose to settle on. If we have no plans, then our faith is small and therefore, we will live on a lower level of supernatural power than His highest will for us.

You see, God has a purpose and a plan for us. But here's the reality: purposes are unchanging, but plans change. This reality is why God will work bad things for our good and His glory. God in His unchanging purpose for our lives will constantly work within the ever-changing fluidity of our world to accomplish His will. He does not plan bad things for us but uses bad things for our good.

So, the heart behind the second statement is to understand that God does not promote lazy or entitled children. It is one thing to expect divine favor to be added to what you bring to the table. It is another thing entirely to expect divine favor to be given when you bring *nothing* to the table. One heart posture does not take God's favor for granted while the other has been deceived into believing God will do everything for them.

And if you're going to rule on earth as God rules in Heaven, you will need to be in partnership with Him as opposed to just being the beneficiary of all of His blessings. The way you do that is by doing the following:

1. Set aside one whole day for just you and God – no distractions, obligations, etc. (or one 2-hour block of time if you have a family)

2. Sit with a pen and a notebook

3. Take 10 minutes and ask the Holy Spirit to show you His final intention for your life
   ** Recommended with your eyes closed **

4. Begin to take the rest of the time to plan out your life – in great detail – what you will do, and what you will need to

see the intention come to fruition. I encourage you to break it down from wide-to-narrow.

** Recommended: Start with decades, then the years within the decades, and the months within the year. **

This planning process with God will be hard, exhausting, and frustrating, but once completed, you will sense a rush of peace, clarity, and strength like none other. That is exactly what happened to me when I planned the next 50 years of my life over a four-hour period. I needed multiple 20-minute breaks in between, but once I finished it, I sensed the Father's smile saying, "I'm proud of you. That was hard, but *we* did it."

It then provided the passion and clarity I desperately needed in order to truly fulfill the dominion mandate over my life. This book is one of the things written on that plan. When you begin the planning process, I would encourage you to do it with the mindset of planning with *pencil*, not *pen*. The reason why is because we must develop the flexibility to hear the Holy Spirit redirect our plans as we are moving forward.

I never knew this book would become more than a book when I first made the plan, but everything changed once my eyes were opened to the weight of it and how it would change my life and many others. The adjustment was not easy at first, because my mind was fixed on what I originally wrote down, but after a few wrestling matches with God, I surrendered. It was in that moment I took to heart this lesson: when you try to win against God, you end up losing, but when you are willing to lose against God, you end up winning. Once you are able to create the blueprint for your life, then you can move to the next step.

2. Study those who are already living in dominion.

Before we ever take the final step of execution, we must study those who have already subdued the area you're called to rule in. Does this mean we only stick to Christian sources? Absolutely not. Does this mean we give preference to Christian voices? Absolutely.

There is a truth we all need to grasp for us to feel peace about moving forward with this second step: the call to rule and have dominion is not just relegated to Christians, but to *all human beings*. The reason is simple: all of us have come from Adam in some family line, and God's dominion mandate

191

was for all of mankind. This truth is self-evident when there are people who aren't followers of Christ subdue their health and reverse diseases or make money work for them instead of them working for money.

The unfortunate reality is that the children of God exercise their rulership birthright far less than those who aren't citizens of the Kingdom. That is one of the primary reasons I wrote this book – to reawaken the king or queen inside every citizen of Heaven.

What is encouraging, however, is that if we choose to become great managers and subdue our lives to follow Christ's rule, the results we experience will have an exponential effect as opposed to an incremental impact. It is likened to two people putting in the same number of hours, and one of them receives double the number of blessings as the other person. That is what divine favor of the Family produces. Even consider this surprising, yet promising verse in Proverbs 13,

> A good man leaves an inheritance to his children's children, but the wealth of the sinner is stored up for the righteous. (Proverbs 13:22, NKJV)

It may seem unusual when the beginning of the verse speaks about a good man leaving an inheritance and then say in the next breath that the wealth of the wicked will transfer over to the righteous. But here's the wisdom of Solomon about it: if you are able to leave an inheritance for your grandchildren while you are still alive, then that means you have made money your servant instead of it being your master.

Think about it in practical terms. How much money will you have if it covers you and your spouse's needs and wants, your children's wants and needs, and still have so much leftover that it covers your grandchildren's wants and needs? If it's not clear yet, that's a *lot* of money.

When you righteously rule over money the way Jesus commands, through proper management and radical generosity, then when the tactics of the wicked catch up to them, the money they lose as a result is handed over to those that are trustworthy enough to manage it well - hence the righteous!

The reason this great transfer of wealth hasn't occurred yet is because the Church as a whole has yet to rule money the way we were designed to. We do not lead because we are not studying those who have taken dominion over it, mainly because they aren't a follower of Jesus and we do not want to seem "unspiritual or carnal". But if we are going to enact our rulership birthright over our minds, bodies, emotions, relationships, destinies, etc., then we need to embrace the posture of a student and the curiosity of a child.

So, make the decision today to study those who are already living in dominion. As the expression goes, "Digest the meat and spit out the bones" - take in the good and push out the bad. Success and genius leave clues so don't miss them while they are in front of you.

Once you study other people who are exercising their rulership birthright and formulate tips or techniques to move forward along with your well-formulated plan, you can then press onto the third and final step.

3. Execute your plan by managing your time and energy.

Plans are powerful expressions of faith because there's a feeling of certainty once you write it down, but this is the

194

reality: developing the plan and identifying the proper tactics means nothing without execution.

If you do not take what has been written down and bring it into the world, then you are not ruling like your Father. This is shown in Genesis when the Creator creates something out of nothing. It is seen when He fashions the material world from the immaterial world. He takes the plans in His heart and brings it out into the world.

Ideas, plans, and purposes are the same. When an idea comes into your mind or an awareness of your purpose is actualized, it is an invitation to form something out of nothing. It is an opportunity to partner with the Holy Spirit to grab what is in the spiritual realm and birth it into the physical realm. This book is a perfect example.

As I began studying the Scriptures slowly during the pandemic, it caused me to notice things I missed when I was in a rush and the Holy Spirit prompted me to bring these spiritual truths into this physical world as a digital, audio, or physical product. I took what He showed me in the realm of Heaven and brought it into the realm of earth through dedicated execution. And it is for this chief reason why you must seek to execute this plan and tips without regards to distraction or plain busyness.

For you to be able to fully take advantage of your birthright, there needs to be a parting with the old way of thinking as it pertains to activity. Being effective is much greater than being efficient. The purpose of execution is not about fitting more into your day but doing more of the things you're supposed to do. You do this by eliminating activities that you do to seem busy and start doing the things that fulfill your purpose.

Your ability to execute will begin to flourish when you rule over two things: your time and energy.

As it pertains to your time, it is the only resource in your life that is non-renewable. In other words, once you use it, you cannot get it back. Usually, when people are young, they trade time for money, but as they grow older, they trade money for more time on this earth. They pay thousands of dollars without hesitation to maintain or recoup their health. They complete the trade so they can fly across the country to hold their grandchildren. Moses even knew the importance of time as he prayed this line in Psalm 90,

> So teach us to **number our days**, that we may gain a heart of wisdom. (Psalm 90:12, NKJV)

Time is the one resource every human being wants more of and desires to maximize. Many people want more money, but once they reach a specific net worth, they realize the value of their time far exceeds the value of their bank account. Even though time is one of those non-renewable sources, the letter to the Ephesian shares a secret with us about getting the most out of it.

> See then that you walk circumspectly, not as fools but as wise, **redeeming** the time, because the days are evil. (Ephesians 5:15-16, NKJV)

The phrase for "redeem" in verse 16 is *exagorazo*, which is a marketplace term for "buying up." When you look at the context of the verse and go deeper, you will discover that it directly means "to buy back." In essence, Paul was telling the Ephesian Church that if they lived wisely and took their time seriously, they *could buy back the time they lost* and save up for more. Essentially, if you master your time, you master your life.

And the vital reality I want to encourage you in is that there are two equalizers among mankind: the blood of Jesus and time. The blood of Jesus puts every person on equal ground in His Kingdom because all of us deserved wrath. God's wrath was not based on race, socioeconomic class, upbringing, or gender. He based it only on sin and that is precisely why, once we receive grace through faith in His sacrifice, we are all on equal ground (Gal. 3:28).

Time works the same way. Whether you live in a mansion or you live in an RV, you have been entrusted with 24 hours in a day. If you travel all of the time or never leave your hometown, you have the same hours. And whatever equalizes all of mankind and unifies us, we should never trample it underfoot nor treat it lightly. God understands how precious the blood of Jesus and time are because we are judged on, first and foremost, whether we accepted or rejected the Cross – salvation – and then after that, how we lived our lives with the 24 hours a day we were given that add up to the totality of our lives – eternal rewards.

Now onto the practical actions: Go to the store and buy either a planner or a composition notebook. Then before you go to sleep, write out what tomorrow will look like in one-hour increments. Do not use the same notebook you created your life plan on as it is best to not cloud one notebook with multiple subjects. Then, as you go throughout your day, continually check your progress. It's hard to hack your time if you don't track your time. As we discussed earlier, you know you are serious about ruling your time when you plan it out.

Now, it does us no good if we are planning our day but have no energy to carry it out. Low energy is a sign that you have not taken the necessary steps to subdue your body. If you are out of shape, eat tons of sugar, and allow toxic people into your life, then it becomes easy to not be motivated enough to rule your day.

There are plenty of books out there about the importance of exercise and healthy foods. Still, I will tackle two things you must filter out of your life: foods that impact your blood sugar and negative/critical people.

Foods that impact your blood sugar cause you to experience that "Sunday nap" sensation. You need to know that food was never meant to cause you to sleep but energize you.

This means guarding against foods with sugar and excess carbs. If you have a hesitation of what you are eating, a simple search on the Internet will show you whether it causes your blood sugar to spike or dip. If you want to cheat, which I struggle with every day, then pick one day out of the week to indulge your sweet tooth. For me, it is on Saturday during my Sabbath that I eat ice cream, cookies, or brownies – or all three at once.

As you cut out the foods that zap your energy and you take more of a conscious effort to subdue your energy, you will notice another influential source coming to steal your power: negative and critical people. Relationships contain a powerful effect to shift people's hearts in dramatic ways. A perfect example is checking your emotions after you leave a family gathering. You either feel completely drained because you spent most of your time with that one uncle who complains the entire time and has nothing good to say about anything or anyone or you feel energized because you were around people who built you up.

Another example of the positive effects that relationships have on us is when my wife is out spending time with her girlfriends at a coffee shop for five hours (husbands know precisely what I'm talking about) and she comes home glowing with joy. It is so noticeable that she seems to float and twirl as she walks in the door (I'm being facetious, but it sure seems that way).

Her words are consistently, "my heart feels full," when she is around the right people. Unfortunately, in the age of social media and instant access, we have given people no boundaries in interacting with us. We let people into our hearts and minds immediately with one comment or direct message. This is not healthy at all if we want to rule our world. The toxic interactions on social media got so bad for me one time that I deleted all the apps off my phone. I never used the "God told me" excuse because I took ownership over that decision.

Some of us need to unplug and focus on the people, responsibilities, and opportunities in front of us instead of the ones "out there." If we took a brutally honest inventory of the value of social media and its allowance for negative and critical people to speak into our lives, we would realize that its value is not much, if any at all.

I did that inventory myself. It wasn't easy, but I was more interested in the truth and ruling than in my comfortable habits. I had the temptation to justify every connection I made, but I knew what the real answer was. I've cut out so many people who did not add to my life, especially those who would critique first rather than ask questions to understand. The ones who know my heart are the ones I've focused on, and this has allowed me to witness God create a breakthrough in them and in me.

This change of focus has even boosted my energy to levels I did not have since I was in high school. I feel more joyful, grateful, at peace, focused, disciplined, and effective ever since I made that switch. My marriage is sweeter than ever, revival is hitting the youth and young adults of our area, and dreams are coming to fruition before our eyes.

Even though it will be hard to cut back from the people you're used to being around, regardless of whether they are negative or critical, just know that there is freedom and strength on the other side. Your ability to rule your heart and master your energy will come much easier when this subtraction occurs. You need to guard your reservoirs of energy because dominion is a combination of time and energy mastery. If you can rule both your time - where every moment counts - and your energy - where you have boundless, strength-filled passion - then you can wage war against the kingdom of darkness and take back your life and our world.

So, there you have it. In order to retrain your hands for dominion, you must create a plan with God about your life, study those who are already living in dominion, and execute your plan by managing your time and energy. Apply these three steps and watch the transformation of your life occur, especially as you combine the steps discussed with renewing your mind and reshaping your heart.

Key Principles

1. If our beliefs and emotions are not properly realigned, then the actions we take with our hands can either be of no benefit or inappropriate.

2. If the Divine Creator suggested an unredeemed Cain should rule over sin, then a fully surrendered and Holy Spirit-filled believer can surely conquer it.

3. God explicitly planned for you to be blessed if you chose to obey His commands wholeheartedly and walk in the identity of the ruler you genuinely are.

4. To be more than a conqueror is to be a ruler.

5. Jesus wants you to have peace now in this life and in the life to come.

6. Planning is one of the highest physical expressions of faith towards God.

7. God has a plan for you, but He doesn't plan for you.

8. The reason the great transfer of wealth hasn't occurred yet is because the Church as a whole has yet to rule money the way we were designed to.

9. Success and genius leave clues so don't miss them while they are in front of you.

10. The two things you must rule over to execute effectively is your time and energy.

11. If you master your time, you master your life.

12. It's hard to hack your time if you don't track your time.

13. To master your energy, you must avoid foods that impact your blood sugar and negative/critical people.

14. Dominion is a combination of time and energy mastery.

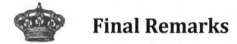

Final Remarks

You are a ruler. You are powerful. You are a king or queen under God. Your birthright is that of a leader, not that of a victim.

As we are concluding our journey together, my heart for you is that your eyes are opened to God's will for you - to rule on earth as He rules in Heaven. My love and care for you to recognize this truth about yourself can be found in the Apostle Paul's heart when he writes to the church in Ephesus,

> that the God of our Lord Jesus Christ, the Father of glory, may give to you the spirit of wisdom and revelation in the knowledge of Him, **the eyes of your understanding being enlightened**; that you may know what is the hope of His calling, what are the **riches of the glory of His inheritance in the saints**, and what is the **exceeding greatness of His power toward us who believe**, according to the working of His mighty power. (Ephesians 1:17-19, NKJV)

As God has placed the burden of this message on my heart, I can't help but experience the exact sentiments shown in the verses above. When you truly grasp the reality that rulership is your birthright and that God wants you to walk in it, it is hard to be ignorant of the exceeding power He amply supplies on our behalf.

After you finish reading to the end of this book, I hope you never see yourself the same way. I hope the person you used to see in the mirror is shattered and replaced by the one who has a crown on their head and a scepter in their hand. That person staring back at you is one with strength in their eyes, love in their hearts, and power in their soul. You need to know this: the person looking back at you has *always* been the real you; you just needed to discover them.

Now that the *present* you has been formally introduced to the *real* you, it is time for you to go about your life making the impact on this world God meant for you. It is time to do what you were born to do - take dominion over your life and then over the world around you. Do it with the heart of having every neighborhood, city, region, state, and nation come under the lordship of our King Jesus.

Nothing can stop you - not Hell, Satan, or others. The only force that can do this is yourself. Still, if you confidently give complete access to the Holy Spirit, you will overcome anything that is thrown your way. So, surrender yourself on a daily basis, rewire your mind to match that of a ruler, reshape your heart to experience your mighty Kingdom life, and retrain your hands to subdue every area of your world.

You were made to be great. You won't fail. After all, you were born to rule.

Appendix- The Full Profile of a Ruler Under God

To be chosen by God, to exercise His delegated authority on earth is a privilege of the highest honor. It cannot be taken lightly nor selectively ignored. You must walk into it with confidence and boldness while also embracing it with reverence. By no means, however, will your growth as a ruler cease even after you accept and begin walking in authority. The steps of learning to live as a child of God and as a king or queen under Him will take the rest of your life.

This means God will never leave you nor forsake you because you are an unfinished work, and He always finishes what He starts (Philippians 1:6). But as you journey with your Father, your identity changes to ultimately reflect Him. Just as a father experiences deep-seated joy whenever his children's actions and attitudes reflect him, so our Heavenly Father experiences that same joy when we do the same.

As we take further steps to rule like God, everything changes. Our minds, hearts, and hands are transformed, and we can never be the same again. In the description that follows, I want you to replace the ruler described with your name as if you are that person. Since you are seated in Heavenly places with Christ, you might as well start seeing yourself that way.

A ruler under God will:

- Be completely surrendered to Christ's rule (Luke 9:23)
- See themselves as the king or queen they are (Revelation 1:5-6)
- Operate with the awareness of God's constant presence as a priest (Revelation 1:5-6; 1 Peter 2:9-10)
- Conquer every negative thought through daily subduing of the mind and performing a negativity fast (2 Cor. 10:4-6; Phil. 4:6-9)
- Love themselves with the same amount God does (Matt. 19:19; John 17:26)

- Take dominion over their health and not allow setbacks to halt their progress
- Refuse to hesitate on listening to someone they disagree with because their end goal is wisdom and truth, not being comfortable (Prov. 2:4)
- Seek to take risks on endeavors that will impact people even if it puts them at an inconvenience (Col. 1:28-29)
- Spend hours perfecting their gifts to a world-class level with the mindset of influencing unsaved rulers (Prov. 22:29)
- Feel wholly secure and bold when amongst influential people in society (Matt. 10:18-20)
- Be more comfortable in the invisible realm of Heaven than the physical realm of earth (Col. 3:1-4)
- Live from a healed and forgiving heart (Eph. 4:32)
- Make the Kingdom and its righteousness their only focus (Matt. 6:33; Prov. 16:12; Prov. 25:5)

- Not allow their passions or lusts to overtake them (Prov. 31:1-4; Eph. 5:15-18)
- Rarely be satisfied until every area of their life is under control - time, money, appearance, health, etc.
- Believe and expect to have a dramatic impact wherever they are (John 14:12)
- Walk in the authority that all of Heaven is inside of you and with you (Eph. 4:19)
- Choose joy and vision over discouragement and despair (James 1:2)
- And much more.

Now remember, you are not going to exhibit all at once every single quality indicated here. That's why this is a journey of rulership *with* Christ. This is mainly a list you can reference back to at any point you need realignment. Creating this list has surely challenged my perspective of myself and I know it will do the same for you.

How you can practically use this list is to write or type it out and make it an "I" statement.

For example,

"I am more comfortable in the invisible realm of heaven and the physical realm of earth" or "I believe and expect to have a dramatic impact wherever I am."

Now go and rule.

Acknowledgments

I would like to acknowledge, first and foremost, my wife and co-ruler, Chantal. Your encouragement to me to stop playing small has pushed me more than ever to run forward with strength and tenacity after the calling over us and our family.

This book and our business are two of those crazy ideas that have come from rejecting the small life. This revelation and understanding of our rulership identity has rocked my world and caused me to desire to dedicate myself to seeing the Body grasp it.

As far my editors, you all know who you are. From both sets of parents (Carlos & Vicky, David & Janelle) to my fellow editors (close to twenty people) to those who were a part of my launch team to those who partnered with us to get this book into many people's hands through your endorsements and getting it translated into other languages to my creative team, I want to say two words that will never do it justice to what you mean to me: thank you.

I mean those two words with every fiber of my being. I am massively grateful for you and am excited to partner with you more for life-changing projects as this. In the meantime, Chantal and I will keep dreaming, working, praying, fasting, learning, and taking risks.

About the Author

Christian Santiago is the CEO of *Born To Rule Global*, a company dedicated to eradicating false humility within the Body of Christ by introducing believers to their rulership identity through books, e-courses, coaching, live events, and products. He is the author of two books, *Lost In Translation: Returning Back to the Original Message of Jesus* and *Detour: When You Feel Like You've Missed Something*.

He has been heavily involved in several areas of ministry within the church ranging from small groups to missions to youth & young adults to children. Him and his wife's life mission is to reawaken every King and Queen buried inside of every child of God.

His wife, Chantal Santiago, is from Australia and they met in the Dominican Republic on a 1Nation1Day mission trip in 2015. They married in April the following year and have been happily married ever since.

If you'd like to reach Christian to bring him to speak to your business team about practically applying rulership to their role, to preach at your church or conference, or have him personally coach you with his Born To Rule High Performance Coaching, you can email him at **christian@borntorule.global.**

CPSIA information can be obtained
at www.ICGtesting.com
Printed in the USA
FSHW011928271220
77025FS